The Penalty of Eve

American University Studies

Series IV
English Language and Literature

Vol. 6

PETER LANG
New York · Berne · Frankfurt am Main

Gladys J. Willis

The Penalty of Eve
John Milton and Divorce

PETER LANG
New York · Berne · Frankfurt am Main

Library of Congress Cataloging in Publication Data

Willis, Gladys J., 1944–
   The Penalty of Eve.

   (American University Studies. Series IV, English Language and Literature; vol. 6)
     Bibliography: p.
     1. Milton, John, 1608–1674 – Knowledge – Manners and Customs. 2. Divorce in Literature. 3. Marriage in Literature. 4. Milton, John, 1608–1674. Doctrine and Discipline of Divorce. 5. Augustine, Saint, Bishop of Hippo. De Doctrina Christiana. 6. Divorce – Biblical Teaching. I. Title. II. Series.
   PR3592.D57W5   1984   821'.4   83-49352
   ISBN 0-8204-0094-7
   ISSN 0724-1453

CIP-Kurztitelaufnahme der Deutschen Bibliothek

Willis, Gladys J.:
The Penalty of Eve: John Milton and Divorce / Gladys J. Willis. – New York; Berne; Frankfurt am Main: Lang, 1984.
   (American University Studies: Ser. 4, English Language and Literature; Vol. 6)
   ISBN 0-8204-0094-7

NE: American University Studies / 04

PR
3592
.D57
W5
1984

© Peter Lang Publishing, Inc., New York 1984

All rights reserved.
Reprint or reproduction, even partially, in all forms such as microfilm, xerography, microfiche, microcard, offset prohibited.

Printed by Lang Druck, Inc., Liebefeld/Berne (Switzerland)

Acknowledgments

Twenty years ago, I was introduced--as an undergraduate--to John Milton's poetry and divorce tracts. The professor to whom I owe many thanks is now deceased. His name was Professor Richard H. Jefferson, Chairperson of the Humanities Department at Jackson State College. This initial introduction sparked a lasting interest which intensified under the tutelage of Professor Maurice Kelley at Princeton University. While personal interest in a subject is important, the encouragement of a respected scholar and friend to pursue the subject is also important. So, I am most grateful to my mentor at Princeton University, Professor Earl Miner, who never wearied of encouraging me to edit my doctoral dissertation for publication. Last and most deserving of thanks is my husband, Andrew, my "Heav'nly Muse."

TABLE OF CONTENTS

Chapter

I.	Introduction..............................	1
II.	St. Augustine's Definition of <u>Caritas</u>.....	11
III.	The Rule of Charity in Milton's Divorce Tracts.............................	29
IV.	Marriage, Divorce, and Reconciliation in <u>Paradise</u> <u>Lost</u>.......................	77
V.	Divorce in <u>Samson</u> <u>Agonistes</u>..............	109
VI.	Conclusion...............................	131
	Notes....................................	139
	Bibliography.............................	153

I
Introduction

John Milton's <u>Doctrine</u> <u>and</u> <u>Discipline</u> <u>of</u> <u>Divorce</u>, along with <u>Tetrachordon</u>, has been the subject of numerous books and papers wherein one finds much subjective biographical commentary directed toward what has been suspected to have been an inharmonious marriage between John Milton and his junior bride, Mary Powell. The purpose of this book is not to make any contribution to this trend of thought, but, rather, to offer a more objective rationale for Milton's divorce tracts. The closest one ever comes to an objective interpretation of Milton's divorce tracts are the few studies on Milton's hermeneutics to which I shall refer later in the text, in more detail. These studies clarify Milton's theory that there are no contradictions of Biblical scriptures, a theory based on the doctrine of analogy. To explain Milton's "rule of charity" and its application to divorce justification - as I expect to do in subsequent chapters - one needs to have some knowledge of Milton's application of the doctrine of analogy.

Although hermeneutics studies have supplied Milton criticism with some welcomed scholarly objectivity, these studies have not sufficiently explained the striking resemblance of Milton's application of the "rule of charity" to marriage to St. Augustine's exegesis of <u>caritas</u> (charity) as the rule of life for every Christian man. The similarities between Milton's method and St. Augustine's exegesis are profound. The problem, however, is the fact that Milton never recorded having read St. Augustine's <u>De</u> <u>Doctrina</u> <u>Christiana</u>, the primary work in which St. Augustine presents his exegesis. When one begins to doubt the probability of St. Augustine as Milton's source, one is even more puzzled by the fact that Milton gave one of his works the very same title as that of St. Augustine's work - De Doctrina Christiana - and wrote it in Latin. But, even in the absence of solid proof, the probability that Milton knew St. Augustine's De Doctrina Christiana is unquestionable. In the preface of his own De Doctrina Christiana, Milton makes general reference to others who had written on the subject of Christian doctrine. It is improbable that Milton would have excluded St. Augustine, the one Church father who continued to influence scriptural interpretation during the Renaissance and Seventeenth Century - despite his association with the Medieval Period:

> I entered upon an assiduous course of study in my youth, beginning with the books of the Old and New Testament in their original languages and going diligently through a few of the shorter systems of divines, in imitation of whom I was in the habit of classing under certain heads whatever passages of Scripture occurred of extraction, to be made use of hereafter as occasion might require.[1]

Based on James Holly Hanford's commentary on Milton's Commonplace Book, Milton did read St. Augustine's De Civitate Dei.[2]

While Milton's Commonplace Book does not provide any proof that Milton read St. Augustine's De Doctrina Christiana, it does not diminish the probability that Milton did know this very important work by St. Augustine. On the contrary, it increases the probability. In his study of the Commonplace Book, Hanford found that "Milton did not record in the volume notes from works to which he must constantly have been referring. There are only three quotations from the classics and none at all from the Scripture. Nor did he ordinarily . . . use it for materials gathered in the immediate process of research, but, rather, as a permanent aid to his thought and memory."[3] Milton, one who was most interested in Church doctrine and theology, must have known about St. Augustine's works years before 1650, the year he recorded as when he read De Civitate Dei.[4]

Despite the premise of "Milton's essential independence and in the absence of records to connect him with numerous authorities,"[5] I find that Milton's "rule of charity" encompasses the basic ideas that St. Augustine presented in his De Doctrina Christiana and further in other of his works, e. g. Enchiridion de Fide, Spe et Charitate and In Joannis Evangelium. From St. Augustine's fundamental exegesis of caritas, Milton could easily design his argument around charity and the "unfit wife." Milton's major emphasis is that charity (love) is Christ's primary commandment to the Christian. According the Matthew 5:17, Christ came to fulfill the Law, not to destroy it. The Mosaic law taught men to love God (Deuteronomy 6:5) and to love their neighbor (Leviticus 9:18); but when Christ came, He taught men not only to love, but He gave them the source of strength within that made them able to follow willingly the commandment, rather than unwillingly - because of forced obedience as a result of fear. Christ taught no differently than did the Mosaic law, except that He taught men that loving one's neighbor is the fulfillment of the whole law. Milton is a firm believer in the new commandment of fulfillment; but he also believes that, to obey consistently this commandment, a man must be kept in a certain frame of mind which is conducive to charity. It follows, then, that whatever inhibits this state of mind is not of God and must be dismissed as immoral, unspiritual, uncharitable and purely detrimental.

Among those scholars who think that it is unlikely that St. Augustine's exegesis of caritas might have been the basis of Milton's "rule of charity," the first is Theodore L. Huguelet. In his book, Milton's Hermeneutics: A Study of Scriptural Interpretation in the Divorce Tracts, Huguelet concerns himself with Milton's use of the "rule of charity" as a means of interpreting the Bible on the subjects of marriage and divorce. In the Seventeenth Century, there was an existing doctrine of analogy, that is using one scripture to explain a more difficult scripture. It is quite evident that Milton believed in this method of interpretation.[6] Huguelet reminds us that St. Augustine referred to the usage first and that, according to St. Augustine, "Every pure hearted Christian who understands that charity is the fulfillment of every command . . . may approach the books of the Bible secure in the understanding of them."[7] This is what St. Augustine taught, but, says Huguelet, "There is no evidence to indicate that Milton got his idea of interpreting by analogy with charity from St. Augustine's <u>De doctrina christiana</u>, a work he nowhere mentions. He apparently felt that he had discovered the key to the Gospel in the analogy of charity - a simple, natural method consistent with the simplicity of Christian doctrine and with the duty of even humble men to search the Scriptures."[8] A probability to the contrary of Huguelet's argument does exist.

Huguelet dismisses the whole issue by saying that "the hint from Grotius, combined with a previous assimilation of Ramistic method, may have been the catalyst which enabled Milton to see the law of charity as a principle of hermeneutics - as, in fact, the key to the Scriptures."[9] The fact that Milton mentions only Grotius is not proof enough to dismiss the high probability that St. Augustine's <u>De Doctrina Christiana</u> might have been the primary source of Milton's understanding and application of the "rule of charity" not only to scriptural interpretation but to the marriage institution and divorce justification. Milton refers to Grotius as "a man of general learning."[10] and, as such, Grotius might very well have been the catalyst that led Milton back to any previous knowledge of St. Augustine that Milton had acquired. It is without doubt that the two had much in common: both men were individualists and committed to some type of religious reform. It is safe to say that Grotius was less of a hazzard to Milton's Protestant position, since Grotius was more contemporary - only twenty-five years Milton's senior, but less of an authority than St. Augustine. It has been pointed out by C.A. Patrides that "Milton . . . unhesitatingly rejected human traditions if they happened to conflict with what he considered to be the sense of the Scriptures, yet readily invoked the Fathers if he found them supporting his individual-Protestant interpretation of a particular idea."[11]

The second important study of Milton's divorce tracts was written by James Basil Potts and entitled <u>Milton's Deviations from Standard Biblical Interpretation in the Discussion of Divorce</u>. Potts is in basic agreement with Huguelet regarding the hermeneutical aspect of Milton's "rule of charity." He places Milton in historical perspective wherein emphasis was placed upon the "supremacy of scripture" and upon the fact that "There could be no contradiction between the several parts of the scripture."[12] With these ideas is coupled that of Milton's belief in "The superiority of the Spirit within--as separate and apart from the written word without . . . ."[13] As far as Potts is concerned, Milton's "rule of charity" is simply "a higher principle by which all interpretation is to be judged."[14] This is indeed the way Milton felt; but, until the time of Milton, the "rule of charity" had never been applied to the controversial subjects of marriage and divorce.

It is obvious that Potts and Huguelet are interested in Milton's use of the "rule of charity" as an all-encompassing principle of hermeneutics, in a general sense. My interest, however, lies not in the general interpretation of the Bible by means of charity, but, rather, it lies in the use of charity to interpret the specific passages of scripture on marriage and divorce. It is understood that Milton felt that the Bible should be interpreted with charity as an end,[15] and I am sure that his contemporaries agreed in principle. None of them, though, was as daring as Milton who used his understanding of charity to solve the seeming conflicts between Old Testament and New Testament scriptures on divorce. Obviously, Milton's concerns extend further than just hermeneutics. He wishes to prove, with his "rule of charity," that an "unfit" marriage partner should be divorced by the believing partner because, otherwise, the believing partner's spiritual communion with God(charity) will be hindered. The irony of the whole situation is that those men (churchmen) who opposed divorce and remarriage most had forgotten or ignored the primary rule of the Christian life -- charity. Man's ability to love God and his neighbor is what charity is all about in Milton's mind. Circumstances which hindered this state of mind would certainly interfere with a man's spiritual welfare, and no scripture could oppose or contradict this fact.

Potts perceives "Milton's concept of charity" as "incidentally spiritual." I find this perception somewhat absurd, simply because too many of Milton's writings place an emphasis upon the spiritual -- in varying degrees. Milton is not just concerned with the "temporal good" as an end, but, rather, as the basis of one's spiritual well-being -- the end of which is spiritual communion with God in Heaven. One's life on earth is the temporal testing ground that prepares man for this eternal communion. Just as St. Augustine was concerned with the temporal man's ability to understand God's word as the basis of his spiritual nuturing in a temporal world(the passageway to the spiritual paradise), so was Milton. Potts proves absolutely nothing when he quotes from St. Augustine's <u>On Christian Doctrine</u>, Book I, Chapter 35, regarding the temporal state:

> The whole temporal dispensation for our salvation, therefore, was framed by the providence of God, that we might know the truth and be able to act upon it; and we ought to use that dispensation, not with such love and delight as if it were a good to rest in, but with a transient feeling rather, such as we have towards the road, or carriages, or other things that are merely means.

Every Christian knew that life on earth was temporal. Milton would have known this if he had never heard of St. Augustine. It is St. Augustine's perception of the "temporal dispensation" that attracts Milton. Hence, any attempt by Potts to discredit any association of Milton with St. Augustine on the basis of the spiritual versus the temporal is a weak attempt. The emphasis upon the temporal world as the passageway to the eternal spiritual paradise gives Milton's argument in favor of divorce more credibility.

Hence, the major emphasis of Huguelet and of Potts is that the "rule of charity" is, for Milton, the key to interpreting all scripture. Again, this is the hermeneutical side of the discussion, but it is not the point at which the discussion should stop. Milton brings the "rule of charity" to test in a very vital human and spiritual controversy. It was quite common, I would think, for the Christian to be aware of the edict that bade men love God, themselves, and their neighbors as themselves. What was not so common was the application of this edict as the solution to the debate upon the dissolution of a spiritually incompatible marriage.

While Huguelet and Potts approach Milton from the hermeneutical point of view, George Halkett, in his book entitled <u>Milton</u> <u>and</u> <u>the</u> <u>Idea</u> <u>of</u> <u>Matrimony</u>, concerns himself with the use of Milton's poetry as doctrinaire exempla of Milton's beliefs about marriage and divorce. Halkett states in the preface of his book that he is "mainly concerned with a special question-- the extent to which the ideal of matrimony in Milton's divorce tracts is embodied in <u>Paradise</u> <u>Lost</u>," as well as how the "tracts accept, deny, modify, or exploit popular, and especially Puritan notions of the marriage relationship. Close attention is paid to the wavering correspondences between word and concept in the practical literature of marriage, the best surviving indication of popular attitudes." Halkett concludes that Milton used not just his Puritan background to build his argument, but he used all that would aid his argument for divorce.

Halket's concerns are particularly interesting to me because, contrary to his conclusions, I believe that there is a profound similarity between Milton's philosophy in the divorce tracts and in two of his most important poems -- <u>Paradise</u> <u>Lost</u> and <u>Samson</u> <u>Agonistes</u>. At points, Halkett becomes contradictory. For example, he makes two statements about the relevance of <u>Paradise</u> <u>Lost</u> to the divorce tracts which are in complete opposition to each other. He states that "The relationship between the divorce tracts and <u>Paradise Lost</u> is manifold, since the marriage presented in the poem has moral, dramatic, and symbolic value";[16] but later he remarks, "Like Milton's heterodox theology, which cannot be fitted into the poetry without much pulling and tugging, his heterodox matrimonial views stand apart from the poem, and when they appear they are tempered and altered by the context."[17] This last statement is somewhat confusing, especially when I think of just how closely related the divorce tracts are to <u>Paradise Lost</u> and <u>Samson Agonistes</u>. While Milton's matrimonial views may be viewed as heterodox, these views have been very aptly incorporated into <u>Paradise Lost</u> and <u>Samson Agonistes</u>. This fact becomes more obvious when the Augustinian pattern is followed in Milton's divorce tracts. There is very little "pulling and tugging" that one needs to do, in order to show the correlation between the tracts and the two poems.

From what has been said, it will be clear that there is a need for the Milton student and scholar to go beyond the accepted fact that the "rule of charity" was for Milton the key to scriptural interpretation, for this is not in dispute. It is important to show the uniqueness of Milton's application of the concept in his defense of divorce on Biblical grounds. His defense finds credence in the doctrine of love which has no affinity with human or Christian bondage, such that would hinder a Christian man's total love for Christ. Nowhere in any of Milton's works does he go to such great lengths to stress the significance of charity as the deciding factor in questions relative to divorce as he does in the divorce tracts. Obviously, the "rule of charity" was a given factor which had been accepted as the rule upon which Christians could make decisions in their daily lives; but, on the other hand, the rule became null and void in deciding whether or not divorce was sanctioned by Christ for reasons other than adultery and fornication.

In showing just how relevant the "rule of charity" was in this argument, Milton revealed the theological incompetence of many of his contemporaries who denied that Christ, who taught man to love God with his whole heart, soul, and mind, to love himself, and to love his fellow-man as himself, could have ever sanctioned divorce. Milton's position may be understood in the following syllogism: 1) that which affects a man's charitable nature--the state of mind which allows him to love God with his whole heart, mind and soul, to love himself, and to love his fellow-man as himself--should be divorced; 2) an "unfit" wife affects a man's charitable nature--the state of mind which allows him to love God with his whole heart, soul and mind, to love himself, and to love his fellow-man as himself; 3) an "unfit" wife should be divorced. If the case is vice versa, Milton gave the wife the same right--basically because he knew that such made good sense, but not because he necessarily believed in a wife's right to divorce her husband. The general feeling was that divorce should be a husband's privileged cure for an "unfit" wife and, as such, divorce should be the just penance of an "unfit" wife. This is the one area where Milton's association with twentieth century ends, for his biasness toward the husband's rights as opposed to the wife's rights would meet with much antagonism in present day society-- if not by men, certainly by women. Upon reading the divorce tracts and, then, <u>Paradise Lost</u>, one can easily make the connection between the archetypal "unfit" wife described in the divorce tracts and Eve, Milton's exemplum of this archetypal persona, the representative of all wives who fit into Milton's prescribed mold.

In the divorce tracts, Milton was primarily concerned with Christian ethics and morality as they relate to marriage. The argument centers upon the moral precepts of the Old Testament and those of the New Testament. The moral precepts of the Old Testament are enveloped in the Mosaic laws and certain addenda, whereas the moral precepts of the New Testament are enveloped in the words of Christ. Nevertheless, if Christ came to fulfill the law, all conflicts should have been resolved. Milton's "rule of charity" proved that: it closed the gap between the Old Testament and the New Testament. The specific instructions to love, given to man in the Old Testament, are found in Deuteronomy 6:5 (RSV) and in Leviticus 19:18 (RSV). The former scripture states that "you shall love the Lord your God with all your heart, and with all your soul, and with all your might." The latter scripture states that "you shall love your neighbor as yourself." In the New Testament, the same instructions are given. According to Mark 12: 29-33 (RSV), "'you shall love the Lord your God with all your heart and with all your mind, and with all your strength . . . . you shall love your neighbor as yourself.'" But, in Romans 13: 8-10, one learns that all the commandments "are summed up in one sentence, 'You shall love your neighbor as yourself.' Love does no wrong to a neighbor; therefore love is the fulfilling of the law." Hence, the moral law of the Old Testament could not have been abrogated in the New Testament, for therein Christ gave man that which would help him willingly abide by the precepts of the law. The Mosaic law was no more than a guide to daily living and making moral decision. Divorce could certainly be categorized as a moral and spiritual question.

II
St. Augustine's Definition of <u>Caritas</u>

> Quod vero ita fit vel timore poenae, vel aliqua
> intentione carnali, ut non referatur ad illam
> charitatem quam diffundit Spiritus sanctus in
> cordibus nostris, nondum fit quemadmodum fieri
> oportet, quamvis, fieri videatur.
> De Doctrina Christiana

St. Augustine of Hippo (354-430) has been known as a prominent figure not only in the realms of the Catholic church but also in the early settling of the Protestant church during the Protestant Reformation and later. Much Protestant doctrine came from the works of St. Augustine, the Christian exegete, whose most significant work relative to Christian doctrine is <u>De Doctrina Christiana</u> (<u>On Christian Doctrine</u>). It is in this work that St. Augustine discusses the fundamentals of the concept of charity. Other important works of his on the subject of charity are the <u>Enchiridion De Fide</u>, <u>Spe et Charitate</u> (<u>The Enchiridion on Faith</u>, <u>Hope</u>, and <u>Love</u>) and <u>In Joannis Evangelium</u> (<u>Homilies on the Gospel of St. John</u>).

In <u>De Doctrina Christiana</u>, St. Augustine defines charity as the "motum animi ad fruendum Deo propter ipsum, et se atque proximo propter Deum."[1] The <u>OED</u> defines charity as "1. Christian love: a word representing <u>caritas</u> of the Vulgate, as a frequent rendering of dγάπη in N. T. Greek." There are three basic applications, "a. God's love to man. (By early writers often identified with the Holy Spirit.) b. Man's love of God and his neighbor; commanded as the fulfilling of the Law, Matt. xxii. 37-40. c. esp. The Christian love of our fellowmen; Christian benignity of disposition expressing itself in Christ-like conduct: one of the three Christian graces; fully described by St. Paul, 1 Cor. xii." The exact opposite of charity, according to St. Augustine, is <u>cupidity</u>, the "motum animi ad fruendum se et proximo et quolibet corpore non propter Deum."[2] The <u>OED</u> makes reference to this condition in a fourth application, "e. In, out of, charity: in or out of the Christian state of charity, or love and right feeling towards one's fellow Christians." It is from this clear understanding of charity that St. Augustine is able to establish the criteria for living a spiritual life.

The basis of truth that every mortal being who considers himself a Christian must never forget is that life on earth is a journey toward the eternal life with Christ. Whether or not the journey is a successful one depends upon what one does while on earth, the place where man prepares for the blessed life with Christ. St. Augustine taught that

> sic in hujus mortalitatis vita peregrinantes a Domino, si redire in patriam volumus, ubi beati esse possimus, utendum est hoc mundo, non fruendum; ut invisibilia Dei, per ea quae facta sunt, intellecta conspiciantur, hoc est, ut de corporalibus temporalibusque rebus aeterna et spiritualia capiamus. (Thus in this mortal life, wandering from God, if we wish to return to our native country where we can be blessed we should use this world and not enjoy it, so that the " invisible things" of God "being made" may be seen, that is, so that by means of corporal and temporal things we may comprehend the eternal and spiritual.)[3]

In order to complete the journey, the Christian must distinguish between those "things which are to be loved and enjoyed" and those "things which are to be used." St. Augustine differentiates between the two:

> Illae quibus fruendum est, beatos nos faciunt. Istis quibus utendum est, tendentes ad beatitudinem adjuvamur, et quasi adminiculamur, ut ad illas quae nos beatos faciunt, pervenire, atque his inhaerere possimus. (Those things which are to be enjoyed make us blessed. Those things which are to be used help and, as it were, sustain us as we move toward blessedness in order that we may gain and cling to those things which make us blessed.)[4]

If a man is not constantly aware of the spiritual end, he is bound to err:

> Nos vero qui fruimur et utimur, inter utrasque constituti, si eis quibus utendum est frui voluerimus, impeditur cursus noster, et aliquando etiam deflectitur, ut ab his rebus quibus fruendum est obtinendis vel retardemur, vel etiam revocemur, inferiorum amore praepediti. (If we who enjoy and use things, being placed in the midst of things of both kinds, wish to enjoy those things which should be used, our course will be impeded and sometimes deflected, so that we are retarded in obtaining those things which are to be enjoyed, or even prevented altogether, shackled by an inferior love.)[5]

The mind must be able to distinguish between two kinds of things. Not being able to do this may be compared to the predicament of a man headed to California by plane, but becomes engrossed in the metroliner, forgets his destination and climbs aboard the metroliner which is bound for Alabama. The anticipated blessedness of the end must always overcome the tendency to want to enjoy the excitement of the means. John Burnaby calls our attention to a beautiful example given by St. Augustine:

> That Augustine, for himself, had a profound distrust of all natural pleasures which he was little concerned to disguise, does but increase the significance of the more liberal view which as a Christian teacher he felt bound to maintain. It is summed up in his beautiful figure of the betrothal ring. 'Let not Satan steal a way into your heart, saying as he is wont, "Enjoy God's creature: why did He make it but for your enjoyment?" . . . God forbids not the love of these things (<u>amare</u>), but only the finding of our happiness in the love of them (<u>diligere ad beatitudinem</u>): we are to make the love of their Creator the end of our esteem for them. Suppose, brethren, a man should make a ring for his betrothed, and she should love (<u>diligeret</u>) the ring given her more than her betrothed who made it for her, would not her heart be convicted of infidelity in respect of the very gift of her betrothed, though what she loved were what he

> gave? Certainly let her love (amaret) his gift; but if she should say "The ring is enough, I do not wish to see his face again," what should we say of her? . . . The pledge is given by the betrothed just that in his pledge he himself may be loved. God, then, has given you all these things; love Him who made them.'[6]

Man ought to think of this temporal world as the means and not the end. Again, it is what a man does with this world or what he does in this world that counts.

The most constructive concept in St. Augustine's De Doctrina Christiana is that of "things to be enjoyed" and "things to be used," the former referring to the blessed (the end) and the latter referring to that which leads toward the blessed (the means). It seems that, according to this doctrine, some things might be used and enjoyed at the same time, such as man's fellow-man (including woman). It might seem absurd that one would describe man as a "thing" to be enjoyed and used. But, as a corporal body, man must be used by man as one of the means of reaching the Father. Man must be loved and enjoyed for the God that is seen in him. St. Augustine said:

> Cum autem homine in Deo frueris, Deo potius quam homine frueris. Illo enim fueris quo effeceris beatus; et ad eum te pervenisse laetaberis, in quo spem ponis ut venias. (When you enjoy a man in God, it is God rather than the man whom you enjoy; for you take joy in Him who will make you blessed, and you will rejoice that you have reached Him in whom you place your hope that you may come.)[7]

St. Augustine taught that "quatuor sint diligenda, unum quod supra nos est, alterum quod nos sumus, tertium quod juxta nos est, quartum quod infra nos est (there are four kinds of things which may be loved: first, the kind which is above us; second, the kind which constitutes ourselves; third, the kind which is equal to us; and fourth, the kind which is below us)."[8] This is the sum of the divine commandment which encompasses the moral teaching of charity in the Old Testament and in the New Testament: Man must love God with his whole heart, soul, and mind, himself and his fellow-man as himself. However, in loving or enjoying our neighbor, we must realize that the things which demand our first love are the "Pater et Filius et Spiritus sanctus, eademque Trinitas, una quaedam summa res, communisque omnibus fruentibus ea; si tamen res et non rerum omnium causa sit, si tamen et causa (the Father, the Son, and the Holy Spirit, a single Trinity, a certain supreme thing common to all who enjoy it, if, indeed, it is a thing and not rather the cause of all things, or both a thing and a cause)."[9]

The above clarifications lead us to the reasons that man must be enjoyed or loved as well as used:

> In his igitur omnibus rebus illae tantum sunt quibus fruendum est, quas aeternas atque incommutabiles commemoravimus; caeteris autem utendum est, ut ad illarum perfructionem pervenire possimus. Nos itaque qui fruimur et utimur aliis rebus, res aliquae sumus. Magna enim quaedam res est homo, factus ad imaginem et similtudinem Dei, non inquantum mortali corpore includitur, sed inquantum bestias rationalis animae honore praecedit. Itaque magna quaestio est utrum frui se homines debeant, an uti, an utrumque. Praeceptum est enim nobis ut diligamus invicem; sed quaeritur utrum propter se homo ab homine diligendus sit, an propter aliud. Si enim propter se, fruimur eo; si propter aliud, utimur eo. Videtur autem mihi propter aliud diligendus. Quod enim propter se diligendum est, in eo constituitur vita beata; cujus etiamsi nondum res, tamen spes ejus nos hoc tempore consolatur. (Therefore, among all those things only those are to be enjoyed which we have described as being eternal and immutable; others are to be used so that we may be able to enjoy those. In the same we who enjoy and use other things are things ourselves. A great thing is man, made in the image and likeness of God, not in that he is encased in a mortal body, but in that he excels the beasts in the dignity

> of a rational soul. Thus there is a
> profound question as to whether men
> should enjoy themselves, use themselves,
> or do both. For it is commanded to
> us that we should love one another, but
> it is to be asked whether man is to be
> loved by man for his own sake or for the
> sake of something else. If for his own
> sake, we enjoy him; if for the sake of
> something else, we use him. But I think
> that man is to be loved for the sake of
> something else. In that which is to be
> loved for its own sake the blessed life
> resides; and if we do not have it for the
> present, the hope for it now consoles us.)[10]

Actually, to love someone for the sake of something else is to use that person as a means of attaining something greater, since "Frui enim est amore alicui rei inhaerere propter seipsam" and "Uti autem, quod in usum venerit ad id quod amas obtinendum referre, si tamen amandum est. (To enjoy something is to cling to it with love for its own sake. To use something, however, is to employ it in obtaining that which you love, provided it is worthy of love.)"[11] In this case, that to which one would direct his love is worthy, for He is God. Man is loved for the likeness of God in him, but he, the beloved, is being used at the same time in the journey of the lover toward God. According to I John 4:20 (RSV), "If anyone says, 'I love God,' and hates his brother, he is a liar; for he who does not love his brother whom he has seen, cannot love God whom he has not seen."

In the life of the Christian, charity is vital to spiritual welfare. Without it, man finds that he has violat- all rules of the Christian faith and put his moral life in jeopardy:

> Tunc est quippe optimus homo, cum tota
> vita sua pergit in incommutabilem vitam,
> et toto affectu inhaeret illi . . . Haec
> enim regula dilectionis divinitus
> constituta est: "Diliges," inquit,
> proximum tuum sicut teipsum; Deum vero
> ex tota corde et ex tota anima et ex

> tota mente," ut omnes cogitationes tuas
> et omnem vitam et omnem intellectum in
> illum conferas, a quo habes ea ipsa quae
> confers. Cum autem ait, "tota corde,
> tota anima, tota mente"; nullam vitae nos-
> trae partem reliquit, quae vacare debeat
> et quasi locum dare ut alia re velit frui;
> sed quidquid aliud diligendum venerit in
> animum, illuc rapiatur, quo totus dilec-
> tionis impetus currit. (For he is the
> best man who turns his whole life toward
> the immutable life and adheres to it with
> all his affection . . . . This is the
> divinely instituted rule of love: "Thou
> shalt love thy neighbor as thyself," He
> said, and "Thou shalt love God with thy
> whole heart, and with thy whole soul, and
> with thy whole mind." Thus all your
> thoughts and all your life and all your
> understanding should be turned toward
> Him, from whom you receive these powers.
> For when He said, "With thy whole heart,
> and with thy whole soul, and with thy
> whole mind," He did not leave any part of
> life which should be free and find itself
> room to desire the enjoyment of something
> else. But whatever else appeals to the
> mind as being lovable should be directed
> into that channel into which the whole
> current of love flows.)[12]

One's relationship with his fellow-man can certainly affect his relationship with God:

> Quisquis ergo recte proximum diligit, hoc
> cum eo debet agere, ut etiam ipse toto
> corde, tota anima, tota mente diligat
> Deum. Sic enim eum diligens tanquam seip-
> sum, totam dilectionem sui et illius re-
> fert in illam dilectionem Dei, quae nullam
> a se rivulum duci extra patitur cujus de-
> rivatione minuatur. (Whoever, therefore,
> justly loves his neighbor should so act
> toward him that he also loves God with his
> whole heart, with his whole soul, and with
> his whole mind. Thus, loving his neighbor
> as himself, he refers the love of both to
> that love of God which suffers no stream
> to be led away from it by which it might be
> diminished.)[13]

The question may be asked, to what extent must one love his

neighbor? or what does it mean to love your neighbor as yourself? St. Augustine gave the answer:

> Item amplius alius homo diligendus est
> quam corpus nostrum: quia propter Deum
> omnia ista diligenda sunt, et potest
> nobiscum alius homo Deo perfrui, quod
> non potest corpus; quia corpus per
> animum vivit qua fruimur Deo. (Again,
> another man is to be loved more than
> our own bodies; for all of these things
> are to be loved for the sake of God,
> and another man can enjoy God with us
> while our bodies cannot do this, for the
> body has life only through the soul by
> means of which we enjoy God.)[14]

The idea implied is that we love other men because we desire that they enjoy God as we do.

A close look at St. Augustine's doctrine of charity reveals some Platonic inferences, that is, ideas derived from the conception of Platonic love. We do know that St. Augustine, in his <u>Confessions</u>, Book VII, Chapter XX, refers to his reading of "the Platonists" from whom he was "taught to search for incorporeal truth." The connection becomes clear in the analysis of St. Augustine's understanding of Christian love, especially in his explanation that the love of Christians for each other is so intensely directed toward the source of all love, God. Platonic love involves specifically the spiritual and intellectual being of men--the intellectual and spiritual beings of two persons are so intensely involved until they bypass the carnal and cupidinous in search of the heavenly. Edmund Spencer beautifully describes this Christian love, which is akin to Platonic love, in "An Hymne of Heavenly Love." The "sage and serious" Spenser, as Milton called him, wrote:

> Love, lift me up upon thy golden wings,
> From this base world unto thy heavens
>   hight,
> Where I may see those admirable things
> Which there thou workest by thy soveraine
>   might,

>   Farre above feeble reach of earthly sight,
>   That I thereof an heavenly hymne may sing.[15]
>   (ll. 1-7)

St. Augustine's concept of charity carries with it some aspects of Platonic love, a love of the mind (soul) as the key to man's love for his fellow-man. Such love is a feast of the soul, the rising above "this base world unto" the "heavens hight." Spenser also notes that this process of "rising above" automatically includes charity, for he said, "How can we thee requite for all this thy good?" For the shedding of his blood, Christ only asks that man love Him in return and this love of God branches out to the love of mankind:

>   Then next, to love our brethren, that were
>   made
>   Of that selfe mould and that selfe Makers
>   hand
>   That we, and to be the same againe shall fade,
>   Where they shall have like heritage of land,
>   How ever here on higher steps we stand;
>   Which also were with selfe same price re-
>   deemed
>   That we, how ever of us light esteemed.[16]
>   (ll. 197-203)

Once man comes near heavenly beauty, he has a frame of mind newly cleansed and purified. This state of being is descriptive of that in which man finds himself as he completes his journey toward the Creator--the journey that St. Augustine talks so much about in <u>De Doctrina Christiana</u>. As Spenser describes it, the joy is inexpressible:

>   Then shalt thou feele thy spirit so possest,
>   And ravisht with devouring great desire
>   Of his deare selfe, that shall thy feeble
>   brest
>   Inflame with love, and set thee all on fire
>   With burning zeale, through every part
>   entire,
>   That in no earthly thing thou shalt de-
>   light,
>   But in his sweet and amiable sight.[17]
>   (ll. 267-273)

Even a man's thoughts change:

> Then shall thy ravisht soule inspired bee
> With heavenly thoughts, farre above hu-
>   mane skil,
> And thy bright radiant eyes shall plainely
>   see
> Th' idee of his pure glorie present still
> Before thy face, that all thy spirits shall
>   fill
> With sweete enragement of celestiall love,
> Kindled through sight of those faire things
>   above.[18]   (ll. 281-87)

These lines from Edmund Spenser illustrate where the journey on earth leads, if the Christian man follows charity in all that he does.

Man's love for his fellow-man is rooted in his first love for God, with whom he hopes to have eternal communion at the end of the journey. The process cannot be completed without charity. The spiritual communion that man has with his fellow-man is the joy that each has in his salvation through Christ and in the satisfaction of the hope of a future eternal life with Christ. The common denominator is the love that each man has for God, which permits each man to see God in his fellow-man. Spenser's description of that love which satisfies the soul stems from Plato, who wrote in his <u>Symposium</u> about love between people--a love that is intellectual and philosophical rather than fleshly and a love that is "something . . . which the soul of either evidently desires and cannot tell, and of which she has only a dark and doubtful presentment."[19]

As St. Augustine explains it, charity (<u>caritas</u>) is that which unifies mankind in the journey toward the Creator. He reiterates his basic idea:

> Omnium igitur quae dicta sunt, ex quo
> de rebus tractamus, haec summa est, ut
> intelligatur Legis et omnium divinarum
> Scripturarum plenitudo et finis esse dilectio
> rei qua fruendum est, et rei quae nobiscum ea
> re frui potest; quia ut se quisque diligat,
> praecepto non opus est. Hoc ergo ut nossemus

> atque possemus, facta est tota pro salute
> nostra per divinam providentiam dispensatio
> temporalis, qua debemus uti, non quasi man-
> soria quadam dilectione atque dilectatione,
> sed transitoria potius, tanquam viae, tanquam
> vehiculorum vel aliorum quorumlibet instrumen-
> lorum vel aliorum quorumlibet instrumentorum,
> aut si quid congruentius dici potest ut ea
> quibus ferimur, propter illud ad quod feri-
> mur, diligamus. (The sum of all we have
> said since we began to speak of things thus
> comes to this: it is to be understood that
> the plentitude and the end of the Law and of
> all the sacred Scriptures is the Love of a
> Being which is to be enjoyed and of a being
> that can share that enjoyment with us, since
> there is no need for a precept that anyone
> should love himself. That we might know this
> and have the means to implement it, the whole
> temporal dispensation was made by divine
> Providence for our salvation. We should use
> it, not with an abiding but with a transitory
> love and delight like that in a road or in
> vehicles or in other instruments, or, if it
> may be expressed more accurately, so that we
> love those things by which we are carried
> along for the sake of that toward which we
> are carried.)[20]

It is very important to remember that St. Augustine, as the trend was in his time, took much from classical philosophy that was good and applied it to Christianity. We know that the concept of Platonic love does not compare point for point with the Christian doctrine of charity, but there are those aspects, as mentioned, which do compare. The end of charity is "a love of God and a love of our neighbor."[21] The Christian must be led to charity in all that he does and St. Augustine concludes that

> Quisquis igitur Scripturas divinas
> vel quamlibet earum partem intellexisse
> sibi videtur, ita ut eo intellectu non
> aedificet istam geminam charitatem Dei
> et proximi, nondum intellexit. Quisquis
> vero talem inde sententiam duxerit, ut
> huic aedificandae charitati sit utilis,
> nec tamen hoc dixerit quod ille quem
> legit eo loco sensisse probabitur, non
> perniciose fallitur, nec omnino mentitur.

(Whoever, therefore, thinks that he
understands the divine Scriptures or
any part of them so that it does not
build the double love of God and of
our neighbor does not understand it at
all. Whoever finds a lesson there useful in the building of charity, even
though he has not said what the author
may be shown to have intended in that
place, has not been deceived, nor is
he lying in any way.)[22]

In <u>The Enchiridion on Faith, Hope, and Love</u>, St. Augustine further clarifies what he means by charity. He introduces an added dimension: the love which man must have for God, for himself, and for his neighbor is given to him by the Holy Spirit. This love is greater than faith or hope:

Jam porro charitas, quam duabus istis,
id est, fide ac spe majorem dixit Apostolus,
quanto in quocumque major est, tanto melior
est in quo est. Cum enim quaeritur, utrum
quisque sit homo bonus, non quaeritur quid
credat, aut speret, sed quid amet. Nam
qui recte amat, procul dubio recte credit
et sperat: qui vero non amat, inaniter
credit, etiamsi sint vera quae credit, inaniter sperat, etiamsi ad verum felicitatem
doceantur pertinere quae sperat: nisi et hoc
credat ac speret, quod sibi petenti donari
possit ut amet. Quamvis enim spenare sine
amore non possit, fieri tamen potest ut id
non amet, sine quo ad id quod sperat non
potest pervenire. Tamquam si speret vitam
eternam . . . et non amet justitiam, sine
qua nemo ad illam pervenit . . . . Nam sine
Dei dono, id est, sine Spiritu sancto, per
quem diffunditur charitas in cordibus nos-
tris, jubere lex poterit, non juvare. (And
now as to love, which the apostle declares
to be greater than the other two graces,
that is, than faith and hope, the greater
the measure in which it dwells in a man,
the better is the man in whom it dwells.
For when there is a question as to whether
a man is good, one does not ask what he
believes, or what he hopes, but what he
loves. For the man who loves aright no
doubt believes and hopes aright; whereas
the man who has not love believes in vain,
even though his beliefs are true; and hopes
in vain, even though the objects of his hope

> are a real part of true happiness; unless,
> indeed, he believes and hopes for this, that
> he may obtain by prayer the blessing of love.
> For, although it is not possible to hope with-
> out love, it may yet happen that a man does
> not love that which is necessary to the
> attainment of his hope; as, for example, if
> he hopes for eternal life . . . and yet does
> not love righteousness, without which no one
> can attain to eternal life . . . . For with-
> out the gift of God, that is, without the
> Holy Spirit, through whom love is shed abroad
> in our hearts, the law can command, but it
> cannot assist.)[23]

Without love, there can be no faith or hope, and belief without love profits nothing. It is love for God and his fellow-man that leads man toward the fulfillment of his hope for eternal life. The last part of the above quotation is of special importance in the discussion of the Mosaic law and the Gospel. Love, the Holy Spirit's gift to mankind, assists men in obeying the commandment of the Old Testament--love God with your whole heart, soul, and mind--and the commandment of the New Testament, love your neighbor as yourself, which is the fulfillment of the whole law. This concept of the relationship between the two testaments is crucial to Milton's argument, and particularly in his unusual interpretation of Matthew 5: 31-32.

Milton could only have applauded a major generalization of St. Augustine:

> Omnia igitur praecepta divina referuntur
> ad charitatem, de qua dicit Apostolus: "Finis
> autem praecepti est charitas de corde puro, et
> conscientia bona, et fide non ficta." Omnis
> itaque praecepti finis est charitas; id est, ad
> charitatem refertur omne praeceptum. Quod vero
> ita fit vel timore poenae, vel aliqua intentione
> carnali, ut non referatur ad illam charitatem
> quam diffundit Spiritus sanctus in cordibus
> nostris, nondum fit quemadmodum fieri oportet,
> quamvis, fieri videatur. (All the commandments
> of God, then, are embraced in love, of which
> the apostle says: "Now the end of the command-
> ment is charity, out of a pure heart, and of a
> good conscience, and of faith unfeigned." Thus

> the end of every commandment is charity,
> that is, every commandment has love for
> its aim. But whatever is done either
> through fear of punishment or from some
> other carnal motive, and has not for its
> principle that love which the Spirit of
> God sheds abroad in the heart, is not done
> as it ought to be done, however it may
> appear to men.)[24]

Here the three requirements of a man before charity can exist are clearly stated: "a pure heart," "a good conscience," and "faith unfeigned." If the first two exist, the third is a result, and each state of being exists in relationship to the other. Charity demands a certain state of mind, free of all distractions which make it impossible to love God with the <u>whole</u> heart, <u>whole</u> soul, and <u>whole</u> mind, and one's neighbor as oneself. In such a case, it is hard for man to love himself--when his mind is troubled with an impure heart and a bad conscience. Love for another is thus inhibited and it would be futile to try to worship God in this state of mind.

In the <u>Homilies on the Gospel of St. John</u>, St. Augustine's interpretation of the Holy Spirit as synonymous with charity (love) is continued. A man without charity is in mortal peril:

> Et quomodo corpus tuum sine spiritu, quod est
> anima tua, si fuerit, mortuum est, sic anima
> tua sine Spiritu sancto, id est, sine charitate
> si fuerit, mortua deptuabitur. (And just as
> the body, if it be without Spirit, namely thy
> Soul, is dead; so likewise thy Soul, if it be
> without the Holy Spirit, that is, without
> charity, will be reckoned dead.)[25]

The Christian realizes that the moment he loses love for God, himself, and his fellow-man, his Soul perishes. Charity is necessary for the journey:

> Ut in resurrectione nostra charitas nostra
> flagret, et ab amore saeculi separet, ut
> tota currat in Deum. Hic enim nascimur et
> morimur, hoc non anemus: charitate migremus,

>charitate sursum habitemus, charitate illa
>qua diligimus Deum. Nihil aliud in hoc
>vitae nostrae peregrinatione meditemur,
>nisi quia et hic non semper erimus, et
>ibi nobis locum bene vivendo praeparabimus,
>unde numquam migremus. (In our resurrection
>our love may be inflamed, and may part from
>the love of the world to run wholly towards
>God. For here we are born and die, let us
>not love this world; let us migrate hence by
>love; by love let us dwell above, by that
>love by which we love God. In this sojourn
>of our life, let us meditate on nothing
>else, but that by good living we shall pre-
>pare a place for ourselves there, whence we
>shall never migrate.)[26]

The Christian man abides in the hope of the future. He lives on the promise of God to those who "love Him and grow with the charity of the Holy Spirit."[27]

There are two specifications of charity. First, the love that man has for God and for his fellow-man renews:

>Innovat quippe audientem, vel potius
>obedientem, non omnis, sed ista dilectio
>quam Dominus ut a carnali dilectione dis-
>tingueret, addidit, <u>sicut dilexi vos</u> . . . .
>Dilectio ista nos innovat, ut simus
>homines novi, haeredes Testamenti Novi,
>cantatores cantici novi. (It is not
>indeed every kind of love that renews
>him that listens to it, or rather yields
>it obedience, but that love regarding
>which the Lord, in order to distinguish it
>from all carnal affection, added, "as I
>have loved you." . . . This is the love
>that renews us, making us new men, heirs
>of the New Testament, singers of the new
>song.)[28]

Second, the love that man has for God and for his fellow-man is not a mundane love:

>et qui sancte ac spiritualitu diligit
>promimum quid in eo diligit nisi Deum?
>Ipsa est dilectio ab omni mundana dilec-
>tione discreta, quam distinguendo addidit

> Dominus, sicut dilexi vos. Quid enim
> nisi Deum dilexit in nobis? (he who
> in a honly and spiritual way loveth his
> neighbor, what doth he love in him but
> God? That is the love, distinguished
> from all mundane love, which the Lord
> specially characterized when He added,
> "as I have loved you." For what was it
> but God that He loved in us?)[29]

In this explanation, "sicut dilexi vos," St. Augustine notes that Christ gave of Himself to man because He loved man and desired to see man reunited with the Father. In the same way, men should love one another, the one desiring that the other be in communion with the Son.

> Aimer un autre de toute son âme n'est pas
> se renier ni se sacrifier soi-même, c'est
> aimer autrui comme soi-même, sur pied de
> parfaite équalité. Celui que j'aime est
> mon éqal; je suis l'éqal de celui que
> j'aime, c'est pourquoi je l'aime comme
> moi-même, ainsi d'ailleurs que Dieu l'a
> prescrit. (For another to love with his
> whole heart is not to deny himself or to
> sacrifice himself, it is to love others as
> himself, on grounds of perfect equality.
> He whom I love is my equal; I am the equal
> of him whom I love, this is why I love him
> as myself, moreover as God has prescribed
> it.)[30]

Charity does not mean loving one in order to be reciprocated. Such an idea is fallacious:

> La conception aujourd'hui communément
> repandue que l'idee chretienne de
> charite est une idee vieillie, a la-
> quelle les temps modernes ont
> substitué un idéal de justice, repose
> sur une ignorance complète de la
> doctrine chrétienne telle que
> l'interprète saint Augustin. (The

> conception today commonly widespread that
> the Christian idea of charity is an old
> idea, for which modern times have substi-
> tuted an ideal of justice, rests on a
> complete ignorance of Christian doctrine
> such as the interpretation of Saint Augus-
> tine.)31

The loss incurred in the process of giving of oneself has been a subject for many, but St. Augustine would accept Gilson's interpretation, that "c'est justement en ne vous donnant pas que vous perdriez."32

It is also clear in St. Augustine's teaching that charity and morality are not two separate entities, that is if God requires the giving of the whole individual. As Gilson said:

> Si tel est le caractère absolu de
> son exigence, la charité n'a pas de place
> particulière dans la vie morale de
> l'homme, elle est cette vie morale même.
> Un amour de Dieu qui commence, c'est pour
> l'âme le commencement de la justification;
> que son amour progresse, la justice croit
> d'autant en elle; cet amour devient-il
> parfait, la justice de cette âme est du
> même coup parfaite . . . . un amour de
> Dieu intégralement réalisé se confond avec
> une vie morale intégralement réalisée.
> (If such is the absolute character of his
> unreasonable demand, charity does not
> have a particular place in the moral life
> of man, it is the same moral life. A
> love of God which begins is for the soul
> the beginning of its justification; that
> his love progress, justice believes just
> as much in itself; this love grows to
> perfection, the justice of the soul is
> of the same perfect thrust . . . a love of
> God integrally realized confounds itself
> with a moral life integrally realized.)33

Gilson further states that since "Dieu est charité; la vie morale est charité;" therefore "il faut . . . que Dieu soit en nous, qu'il circule pour ainsi dire en nous, comme une eau vive de laquelle découlent a la fois nos vertus et nos actes. (God is charity; the moral life is charity; [therefore] it is necessary . . . that God be in us, that is to say, that he circulate in us, as a live river from which flows all at once our virtues and our actions.)"[34] This is the means by which man is able to be successful in his journey toward the Father, the "final" hope and end of all his actions on earth.

It is this doctrine of charity upon which John Milton built his concept of charity. Milton is mainly concerned with Christian morality which cannot be divorced from the Biblical teaching of charitable living. As we shall see, this is Milton's ground for extending the doctrine of charity, as St. Augustine explains it, to include the marriage institution, as being the prime example of the marriage between Christ and the church. As a result of this study of St. Augustine, we learn that what has appeared to many to be unorthodox in Milton's divorce tracts turns out to be orthodox in higher or more spiritual terms.

III

The Rule of Charity in Milton's Divorce Tracts

> God preferres the free and cheerful
> worship of a Christian before the
> grievous and exacted observance of
> an unhappy marriage.
> The <u>Doctrine</u> and <u>Discipline</u> <u>of</u>
> <u>Divorce</u>

The subject of divorce was indeed a controversial one four centuries ago and, thus, necessitated the voice of John Milton, "a voice crying aloud" in a wilderness of opposition. Scholars vary in assessing Milton's motives for writing the divorce tracts: there have been those who believed that Milton's interest in the subject of divorce was based upon his own marital problems with his first wife, Mary Powell,[1] while a few others have felt that the divorce tracts were just another phase of Milton's involvement in church reformation and in the fight for individual and domestic freedom of justice;[2] however, Milton describes his interest as follows:

> When the bishops, at whom every man
> aimed his arrow, had at length fallen,
> and we were now at leisure as far as they
> were concerned, I began to turn my
> thoughts to other subjects; to consider
> in what way I could contribute to the
> progress of real and substantial liberty,
> which is to be sought for not from without,
> but within, and is to be obtained princi-
> pally not by [frightening], but by the just
> regulation and by the proper conduct of
> life. Reflecting, therefore, that there
> are in all three species of liberty, with-
> out which it is scarcely possible to pass
> any life with comfort, namely, ecclesiasti-
> cal, domestic, or private, and civil; that
> I had already written on the first species
> and saw the magistrate diligently employed
> about the third, I undertook the domestic,
> which was the one that remained.[3]

When Milton chose to write on this third species, he had something nobler in mind--something nobler than arguing the case of his own marital experience.

In the divorce tracts, Milton set out to establish in the minds of his countrymen the real meaning of marriage, for only after knowing the real meaning of marriage could one understand the moral good of divorce. Milton defines marriage as a spiritual institution wherein spiritual happiness is greatly dependent upon the mental fitness of the wife. One is constantly reminded that the mind of a woman is more important than her body. In the intitution of that Milton describes, the husband is the dedicated follower of God, the head of the wife, and, as such, the spiritual ambassador of the wife--that is, the wife finds salvation through her husband. This understanding of marriage and the assigned roles of the husband and of the wife places the wife in a very important position in relation to her husband. As a helpmeet, the wife comes to be known as a "thing to be used" by her husband in his quest for salvation or for complete union with God. This perspective of the wife as a "thing to be used" finds its pattern in St. Augustine's explanation of <u>caritas</u>.

It has been shown earlier that St. Augustine believed that man's ultimate goal in the physical world should be preparation for the return to his "native country." The believer should progress daily toward this end, as long as he fulfills the commandment of love--to love God above all things. The believer must, at all times, be able to distinguish between "those things to be loved" and "those things to be used." St. Augustine explained that only one thing is to be loved and that is God; and that everything outside of God, if it is to be considered, must be considered a "thing to be used," the category into which man falls. It was St. Augustine's firm belief that when man loves his fellow-man, it is not the man he loves, but the God that he sees in his fellow-man. Thus it is in marriage: the wife is not to be loved as the ultimate end, but rather as one who shares her husband's love of God and constantly nurtures the spiritual relationship. Milton's "rule of charity," as it is presented in the divorce tracts, is built upon this Augustinian doctrine of use. Whether or not divorce is proper and in order can only be decided by answering the question, does the wife aid her husband's spiritual life or does she hinder his spiritual life? If she hinders her husband's spiritual life, then, according to Milton's "rule of charity," divorce is proper and good. If the believing husband is to obey the commandment of love--to love the Lord with his <u>whole</u> heart, <u>whole</u> soul, and <u>whole</u> mind--he must be able to live in a domestic atmosphere of peace and happiness. In Milton's mind, nothing destroys such domestic peace and happiness more than an "unfit" wife.

The Augustinian precepts upon which Milton seems to have built his "rule of charity" become more and more obvious as one follows Milton's argument in the divorce tracts. The key to spiritual growth and well-being in the marriage between believers must be the constant fulfillment of the commandment of love. Milton seems to be more concerned about the spiritual well-being of the husband; but, after all, Milton is a man and he lives in a culture where women are usually thought of as secondary to men. Aside from these facts, Milton had experienced a marriage in which the wife had been the central problem. This is no contradiction of my earlier statement that Milton did not necessarily write the divorce tracts to seek a remedy of his own marital problems. It simply means that Milton is no different than most literary artists: an author's personal experiences provide a frame of reference, just as his social environment does--whether he recognizes it or not. Milton realized that problems can arise on both sides of a marriage. However, because of Biblical and historical perceptions of woman as a follower of her husband, it would have been very difficult for Milton to perceive of woman any differently. From his perspective, the wife should be the husband's helper; but, at the same time, spiritual responsibilities are met through the spiritual communion that she and her husband share together.

Milton was very much alone in suggesting divorce on grounds of spiritual incompatibility; therefore, before discussing any of Milton's divorce tracts, I shall take time to introduce some of the traditional thinking on the subject of marriage with which Milton had to contend. Henre Smith, Robert Cleaver, William Perkins, William Gouge, and Daniel Rogers were among the recognized authorities on the subject of marriage, at least they had been involved enough to write something on the subject. As far as these men are concerned, there is almost unanimous agreement that divorce cannot be granted on grounds other than adultery or fornication, impotence or non-consummation, or desertion. Neither of them is radical enough to oppose Canon law, but each man, in his own way, seems to admit, inconspicuously, much of what Milton has recognized about marital unhappiness and discomfort as reasons that provoke thoughts of separation or divorce. The analysis of these views followed by an analysis of Milton's defense in favor of divorce should place Milton in a more favorable position.

Milton wrote four divorce tracts, but, for the purpose of this study, I shall discuss only two: The Doctrine and Discipline of Divorce (1643, 1644) and Tetrachordon (1643). The remaining two tracts are less important to this study: The Judgement of Martin Bucer Concerning Divorce, published in 1644, was Milton's translation of passages on marriage and divorce from Martin Bucer's De Regno Christi; and Colasterion: A Reply to a Nameless Answer Against The Doctrine and Discipline of Divorce, published in 1645, is a repetition of Milton's original argument. Because of the controversy over the Mosaic Law and the Gospel in relation to the commandment of love and in order to determine the consistency of Milton's views, I have found it necessary to look at passages from Milton's De Doctrina Christiana, which was written later than the divorce tracts, probably between 1656 and 1660. As we move into the discussion of this chapter, we must endeavor to answer two important questions: Was Milton's understanding of marriage so wrong? and Was it not true that tradition and custom were the only stumbling blocks to the real understanding of the fundamental Christian commandment to follow charity in all of one's actions, even in marriage?

Traditional Views of Marriage and Divorce
During the Sixteenth and Seventeenth Centuries
in England

When Milton, in The Doctrine and Discipline of Divorce, began his speech to the Parliament of England by stating that "If it were seriously askt . . . who of all Teachers and Maisters that have ever taught, hath drawn the most Disciples after him, both in Religion, and in manners, it might bee not untruly answer'd, Custome," his wish was to appeal to the logic of his fellow countrymen. The majority of churchmen and lawmakers had failed to found their reasons for opposing divorce upon any rational interpretation of the Scripture. The views of such men as Henry Smith, Robert Cleaver, William Perkins, William Gouge, and Daniel Rogers are indeed informative. Each man, to some extent, became a follower of tradition either by opposing divorce except for the traditional reasons, or by just remaining silent on the matter.

In 1597, a work by Henry Smith (1550?-1591), entitled Preparative to Marriage, was published posthumously. Central to Smith's thesis is the belief that the marriage contract is a very important measure which guards against one's deliberately marrying the wrong person. As far as Smith is concerned, there are three ends of marriage: 1) the procreation of children, 2) the avoidance of fornication, and 3) the avoidance of loneliness. In the divorce tracts, Milton emphasizes the third above the first and second of Smith's ends of marriage. Smith's treatise is more or less a guide for those who intend to be married. In choosing a spouse, one must remember to look for certain qualities:

> To direct thee to a right choise herein, the Holy Ghost gives thee two rules in the choise of a wife, Godliness and fitness: Godliness, that is, graced with gifts, and embrodered with vertues, as if we married holinesse herselfe. For the marriage of man and woman is resembled of the Apostle to the marriage of Christ and the Church. Now the Church is called holie, because she is holie. In the sixt of the Canticles she is called undefiled because she is undefiled. In the 45. Psalme she is called faire within, because her beautie

> is inward: So our spouse should be holy,
> undefiled and faire within. As God respect-
> eth the heart, so we must respect the heart,
> because that must love, and not the face.
> Courteousnesse hath ever been a suter to the
> richest, and pride to the highest, and light-
> ness to the fairest: and for revenge hereof,
> his joy hath ever ended with his wives youth,
> which tooke her beautie with it. The goods
> of the world are good, and the goods of the
> body are good, but the goods of the <u>minde</u>
> [italics mine] are better. As Paul commend-
> eth Faith, Hope, and Charitie, but saith
> the greatest of these is Charity: so may I
> commend beauty, and riches, and godlines, but
> the best of these is godlines, because it hath
> the things which it wants, and makes every
> state alike with her gifte of contentation.[4]

For Smith, the "minde" is of prime importance, as "Godlines" proceeds from the "minde." The mental capacity to commune with God in marriage is a prerequisite of matrimonial harmony or unity. God must be the first love of the couple. In the words of Smith, "Wedlocke is made of two loves, which I maye call the first love, and the after love. As every man is taught to love God before he be bid to love his neighbor; so they must love God before they can love one another."[5]

In the event that there is no mutual love, Smith is not able to suggest any recourse: he said that "unless there be a joining of hearts, and a knitting of affections together, it is not mariage in deede, but in shew and name, and they shall dwell in a house like two poisons in a stomacke, and one shall ever bee sicke of another."[6] When there are marital problems, Smith advises the innocent party to remain and bear the pain. It never occurs to him that to continue an inharmonious relationship is to love matrimony above God. In Augustinian terms, matrimony is not an end but a means. Smith does recognize, however, that mutual love is a necessity in marriage:

> Therefore, first that they maye love,
> and keepe love one with another, it is
> necessarie that they both love God, and
> as their love increaseth toward him, so it

> shal increase each to other. But the man
> must take heede that his love toward his
> wife bee not greater than his love toward
> God, as Adam and Samsons were, for al un-
> lawful love will turne to hatred.[7]

Smith readily agrees that one must love God above everything, including one's wife, but he fails to understand the difficulty of loving God wholly when one's mind is troubled. Smith conforms to the traditional interpretation of Christ's words to the Pharisees on the subject of divorce, sanctioning divorce only on grounds of fornication or adultery.

Robert Cleaver (1562?) published his <u>A Godlie Forme of Householde Government: for the Ordering of Private Families According to the Direction of Gods Word</u> in 1598. The work is important as it makes the husband totally responsible for the salvation of his household, and the wife his aide in fulfilling these responsibilities. There must be, according to Cleaver, "Love and peaceablenesse in the wife towards the husband."[8] Cleaver is among those who feel that marriage is indissoluble:

> The institution of Matrimonie is an indissoluble bond and knot, whereby the husband and wife are fastened together by the ordinance of God, and is straighter then any other coiunction [sic] in the societie of mankinde.[9]

Because marriage is indissoluble, he who intends to marry ought to look for certain qualities:

> Every one therefore that purposeth to marrie, ought also to remember that there be three maner of riches in man. 1. The riches of the <u>minde</u> [italics mine]. 2. The riches of the <u>bodie</u>. 3. The riches of temporall substance. The best and the most precious are the riches of the minde: as without which, the other two are more hurtful then profitable.[10]

So far, Smith, Cleaver, and Milton agree that the mind is the most important attribute to have in a spouse. Cleaver goes further to say that "The riches of the minde, are the feare of God, faith, Gods glorie, knowledge of his will, sobernesse, liberalitie, chastitie, silence, humbleness, honestie, and such like virtues."[11] Cleaver does not, however, suggest divorce except for "whoredome," which is, as was the case with Smith, a result, in Milton's view, of the misinterpretation of the words of Christ to the Pharisees. Keeping what Cleaver has said in mind, one still senses the feeling that he is not so sure that divorce is limited to "whoredome." Cleaver's thoughts are indeed traditional. His only contribution to the divorce controversy is a suggested list of attributes to look for in an intended spouse: "1. The report. 2. The lookes. 3. The speech. 4. The apparell. 5. The companions. 6. and lastly, the education and bringing up, which are like the pulses that shew whether a man be sick or whole, well or ill."[12]

Another point of interest is Cleaver's belief that procreation is the first end of marriage. Accordingly, God gave to some men the "gift of continence," and, to some, "the gift of procreation." If one who has the "gift of continence" marries, his marriage may be dissolved by a "superiour authoritie." Cleaver states that if "naturall frigiditie and coldnes, infancie, incurable diseases" exist and "deprive men of all fitnes for the use of mariage," then the marriage may be dissolved. Of course, it is clear that Cleaver thinks that anything which prevents procreation hinders a harmonious marriage. Milton would disagree. Having stated that procreation is the first end of marriage, Cleaver recognizes the avoidance of fornication as the second end, and the third as "for mans commoditie, to the end to avoid the inconvenience of solitarinesse."[13] Although Cleaver finds it proper to dissolve an unproductive marriage, he has no advice to those husbands and wives who suffer the pain of more intolerable marital problems. Cleaver only shows the courtesy of admitting that there can exist in a marriage vices as well as virtues:

> How, like as in the minde there are virtues, as wee have before spoken of: so are there in it also noysome wicked vices and detractions as ungodliness, despising of Gods word, unbeleefe, idolatrie, superstition, ignorance, churlishnesse, lying, falsehood, hypocrise, unrighteousnesse, swearing, backbyting, mistemperance, drunkennes, glutonnie, covetousnesse, unchastitie, unshamefastnesse, misnourture, rashnesse, furiousnesse, wantonnesse, pride, presumption, vaine-glorie, chiding, brawling, and unhandsomenesse. Why so now chooseth him a wife, or shee a husband, that is infected and tangled with such noysome vices, he seeketh not a spouse, or shee a husband, for a right, peaceable, good, honest, and christian-life; but an hell, a painfulnesse and destruction of all expedient, quiet, and vertous living.[14]

This list includes all that Milton found as reasons for a divorce.

Although Cleaver believes that charity is important in a marriage, he has not found it to be the key to relieving the misery of an unfit marriage. Of the marriage institution, Cleaver said: "But the marriage and company of the husband and wife, is made amiable, sweete, and comfortable, by these five means: by godlinesse, vertue, mutuall forbearing, mutuall love, and by dutifulnesse performed busily and godly on both sides."[15] It would be wise, however, for us to notice the priority that is given to "godlinesse."

> Godlinesse of right, holdeth the chiefe place. For there is no stable & steadfast friendship, unlesse it have his beginning from God: and therefore must godlinesse needs shine before the rest. For when couples have determined to obey God, all things afterward become more easie.[16]

With godliness, there must be charity:

> They ought also each to perswade other
> to charitie, to relieve the poore, diligent-
> ly to frequent sermons, to use praiers and
> supplications, and praise and thanksgiving
> to the Lord, to comfort each other in the
> time of afflictions, to be short either to
> exhort other, to walke in the feare of
> God, and in all duties and exercises beseem-
> ing the children of God.[17]

Charity (love) in marriage is important because

> God commandeth us, to love our neighbours
> as our selves, because they be of our
> flesh. Albeit therefore, that he contemne,
> hate, offend, or wrong us: albeit he be
> our enemie, and in respect of himselfe,
> deserveth not that wee should love him,
> yet because he is of our flesh, the founda-
> tion of love remaineth, wee must love him.
> How much rather ought they put this in
> practise, who by the bond of marriage, are
> made one flesh? The rather, because the
> union betweene man and wife, is without
> comparison more straight & bindeth them
> each to love other, much more then the
> coiunction, whereby man is united unto his
> neighbor.[18]

Having read what Cleaver had to say on the subject of marriage, I find his position rather humorous in the same fashion as Milton found the Canon Law irrational. Cleaver recalls the passage of scripture in the Old Testament where Moses permitted man to divorce his wife on the account of hardness of heart, but Cleaver also quotes the words of Christ in Matthew 19: 8, as a means of discounting the Old Testament record. Cleaver's advice is that, regardless of adverse circumstances in a marriage, the marriage must not be dissolved--except for those cases already mentioned. He said that "the bond of marriage remaineth sted-fast, and [is] not to be dissolved."[19] The two, instead of separating, must "imploy their time in praier."[20] But, Milton would ask,"How can one pray when his mind is not at peace with itself?" Cleaver's response is definite:

> The answere is, that such infirmities must not dissolve, or breake the bond of marriage, and their duties to live together: but let them thinke that God hath called them to the exercise of patience, which upon heartie prayer he graunted to them.[21]

While Cleaver continues to believe that each individual in a marriage must "be a helpe to others salvation," he still does not see where divorce should be granted when godliness does not exist. Cleaver goes far enough to say that a man and wife must not be "hindered, or made slacke in any dutie toward God and their neighbours: as also that no affliction depending or proceeding of marriage, withdraw them, or force them to resolve of anything contrary to the union of marriage, & their christian profession, that they bee the children of God."[22] When reading Cleaver's treatise, one, somehow, gets the feeling that Cleaver sincerely believed that if the right precautions are taken before marriage, there should not be any subsequent problems large enough to necessitate divorce on any grounds other than the accepted ones.

William Perkins (1558-1602) offers more commentary on the subject of marriage in his Christian Oeconomie: A Short Survey of the Right Manner of Erecting and Ordering a Family, According to the Scriptures, which was published posthumously in 1618. Perkins believed that "the happie and prosperous estate of the family, which consisteth in the mutuall love and agreement of Man and Wife . . . dependeth upon the grace and blessing of God: and this blessing is annexed to his worship."[23] Again, the worship of God is of prime importance, although Perkins says later that the ends of marriage are: 1. "procreation of children." 2. "procreation of an holy seed." 3. "to avoide fornication." 4. "that the parties married may thereby performe the duties of their callings, in better and more comfortable manner."[24] Perkins believes that a married man is "much more fit and disposed to meditate on heavenly things, without distraction of mind."[25]

Perkins suggests, as did Cleaver, that certain precautions

be taken before marriage, as a means of insurance. Mistakes are not allowed to be made, except in certain cases. In the event that a man marries an infidel, he has every right to dissolve the marriage. Such thinking brings Perkins closer to the thinking of Milton. Perkins quotes three church fathers--Ambrose, Lombard, and St. Augustine--on the subject. The consensus is that a Christian is not bound to remain married to an unbeliever. The covenant that man has with God is far more important than an earthly marriage. Perkins believes that it is "farre better that the covenant should be dissolved, that man and wife have made each with other, than that the Covenant which man hath made with God."[26] The believer is then free to marry another. The husband has spiritual responsibilities:

> For a husband that is a Christian is maried two waies: First with Christ, and secondly with his wife. The former marriage is made in Baptisme, and is a more holy coniunction, then is the latter. Therefore when these two cannot stand together, but one of them must needes be dissolved; the latter must rather be left than the former. Againe, if the beleever should remaine with the unbeleever, she should haply be urged sometimes, in case of danger upon infirmity, to deny Christ, and make shipwracke of faith and good conscience; which may in no sort be done of either party: and therefore separation is to be made rather in this society, then that the coniunction with Christ should not stand firme, and continue.[27]

It is interesting to note that Perkins says essentially the same thing that Smith has said earlier,[28] in reference to the covenant between man and God, and between man and woman. Perkins sounds quite Miltonic: Milton's basic idea in using the "rule of charity" as his defense in favor of divorce had been that man's first duty is to love God above all things, including matrimony. It must be made clear, however, that even though Perkins sounds Miltonic regarding man's covenant with God, Perkins also follows tradition in believing that marital problems can be avoided if one chooses wisely. Unlike Milton, Perkins' broadmindedness is overshadowed by his traditionalism, which is made obvious by his suggested ends of marriage.

William Gouge (1578-1653), writing in 1622, had more to say about marriage in his Of <u>Domesticall</u> <u>Duties</u>. Gouge appears to be, to some extent, broadminded. He recognizes divorce for desertion, doing so by insinuation:

> In many reformed Churches beyond the seas Desertion is accounted so farre to dissolve the very bond of mariage, as libertie is given to the partie forsaken to marie another and it is also applied to other cases then that which is above mentioned: as when an Infidell, Idolater, or Heretique shall depart from one of the true religion for other causes then hatred of religion: or when both man and wife having lived as Idolators among Idolaters, one of them being converted to the true faith, leaveth his abode among Idolaters, and goeth to the professors of the true faith, but can by no means get the other partie to remove: or when one of the true religion shall depart the same profession, and will by no meanes be brought to live with the partie so left, but openly manifesteth peremptorie obstinacie; the marriage bond may be broken, and libertie given to the party forsaken to marry another. But because our Church hath no such custome, nor our law determined such cases, I leave them to the custome of other Churches.[29]

It may be that Gouge believes in divorce for reasons other than the traditional ones, but does not care to enter the controversy by introducing something different than usual.

Gouge believes in the importance of charity in marriage. Mutual love must exist between husband and wife:

> <u>Love is the fulfilling of the law</u>, that is, the very life of all those duties which the law requireth. It is the bond of perfection, which bindeth together all those duties that passe betwixt partie and partie. Where love aboundeth, there all duties will readily and cherfully be performed.[30]

Love must exist in marriage so that each may be able to perform the first duty to each other, which is to seek "the good of one anothers soule." Gouge further says that to seek this good is "the greatest good that one can possibly doe for another, to be a meanes of helping forward his salvation. And there is nothing that can more soundly and firmly knit the heart on one to another, then to be a meanes thereof."[31] Of the jointure of marriage, Gouge said that "a spiritual edifying of one another is the best use which he can make (and ought to make) of those <u>ioynts</u> and <u>bonds</u> whereby we are knit one to another."[32] The main obstacle to "procuring the <u>Salvation</u> of one another" is "<u>a carelesse neglect thereof</u>: when as husbands and wives minde earthly things as they thinke it enough if they be provident one for another in earthly things of this life."[33] It is obvious that Gouge thinks the temporal life secondary to the spiritual life.

In 1642, Daniel Rogers (1573?-1652) published a treatise entitled <u>Matrimoniall Honour: or, The Mutuall Crowne and Comfort of Godly, Loyall, and Chaste Marriage</u>. Rogers is a firm believer in the importance of unity in religion, the first prerequesite of a happy marriage. The love of God must come first, followed by the love of neighbors. Rogers does not speak extensively on the subject of divorce when there is an unfit partner. He simply refers to the traditional passages of scripture of the New Testament which condemn divorce except for adultery or fornication. He does say, however, that in the event that one finds himself married unwisely, he must

> Rather looke up to God by faith and repentance for your error, that it may be covered, and that Gods anger being removed, you may finde your yoke as tolerable as an unequall one may be. And as once a grave man said to one in his case, if God ever offer you a new choice, beware least you stumble at the stone, which once foiled you.[34]

This passage indicates that one must live with his mistake, and that the only chance of freedom is the death of one's spouse.

Woman is naturally seen as man's helper, but Rogers makes it

clear that there must be mutual concern for the spiritual part
of life. This concern is shown by the fulfillment of certain
duties.

> These duties which concern both
> equally are foure. First, Iointnesse in
> religion; mutuall love; like loyall
> chastity; and sutable consent. Touching
> the first of religion: my meaning is,
> that, as they are entered already with a
> religious spirit, into their marriage,
> so they must continue: not only to be
> religious still, but to cleave mutually
> together in the practice of all such
> meanes of worship, and duties of both
> tables, as concerne them; I say, in the
> parts of religious conversation to God.[35]

This is no more than a command to follow charity in all their
actions. Rogers further teaches that man and wife must worship
both privately and publicly, as on the Sabbath. Both must hear
the Word and receive the sacraments together. They both are
responsible for teaching godliness to their children and to their
servants. Not only are there responsibilities of the two in the
home, but also outside of the home, in the community. Each must,
in unity, participate in

> the duties of charity to the poore, har-
> berousnes to strangers, reliefe of other
> both publique causes and private persons,
> whom by occasion, God offereth to their
> regard.[36]

There must also be

> mutuall harmony in all religious relations,
> both towards themselves, as instruction,
> reproofe, advice, admonition, or encourage-
> ment; or else others, in the Communion of
> Saints . . . or else in the sight of the
> world, which, when it is mutuall, is re-
> sembled in the glasse of each others prac-
> tice, but if not, then looses her beauty
> as we see in the opposition which the Holy

Ghost makes between Abigail and Nabal in that point.[37]

It may be said of Rogers that he thought of religion as "the golden Cement of all fellowships, and unions, both to knit and to sanctifie the same more firmly and closely together."[38] It was for this reason that Milton could use the "rule of charity" to refute the arguments against divorce. Without charity, there can be no spiritual communion in a marriage and one is bound to defy God. A marriage without charity, without the love of God and neighbor, is, in the words of Rogers, "nothing save a fire: a contentious and unpeaceable condition."[39] In spite of the fact that Rogers places religion as a top priority in marriage, he is still a traditionalist in terms of divorce.

The basic fallacy in the thinking of many traditionalists of the sixteenth and seventeenth centuries was to think that a bad marriage could be avoided by making the right choice in the beginning, as if choosing a wife is comparable to purchasing a diamond on the basis of its perfection. Milton's words to men who thought in this fashion were that

> the best and wisest men amidst the sincere and most cordiall designes of their heart doe dayly erre in choosing;[40]

and that

> for all the warinesse can be us'd, it may yet befall a discreet man to be mistak'n in his choice: and we have plenty of examples. The soberest and best govern'd men are lest practiz'd in these affairs; and who knows not that the bashfull mutenes of a virgin may oft-times hide all the unliveliness & naturall sloth which is really unfit for conversation; nor is there that freedom of accesse granted or presum'd, as may suffice to a perfect discerning till too late; and where any indisposition is suspected, what more usuall then the perswasion of friends, that

acquaintance, as it encreases, will amend all.[41]

There is no doubt that Milton's argument in the divorce tracts will be much stronger than the traditional argument against divorce.

The Doctrine and Discipline of Divorce

On the title page of the 1643 edition of The Doctrine and Discipline of Divorce, Milton states his objective as to free men from the bondage of the Canon Law and to guide them "to Christian freedom, guided by the Rule of Charity." On the title page of the 1644 edition, Milton gives some clarification of the "Rule of Charity" as a guide: he declares his intention to free men from the bondage of the Canon Law and to teach them "the true meaning of Scripture in the Law and Gospel compared." Milton felt that if divorce were to be seen ever as a virtue rather than a vice, charity would have to be given its correct scriptural interpretation--"the supreme interpreter" of all Scripture."

> For every act of true faith, as well that whereby we believe the law, as that whereby wee endeavour the law is wrought in us by charity: according to that in the divine hymne of St. Paul, I Cor. 13. Charity beleeveth all things: not as if she were so credulous, which is the exposition hitherto current, for that were a trivial praise, but to teach us that charity is the high governesse of our belief, and that wee cannot safely assent to any precept writt'n in the Bible, but as charity commends it to us.[42]

That man should love God before all things and in all things, including matrimony, is the case that Milton presents. The "rule of charity" gives man the freedom to sever himself from whatever thing or being that hinders his obedience of the commandment of love. While St. Augustine had spoken from a general view of the Christian life, Milton spoke in terms of a specific area of the Christian life--the marriage institution.

The absence of charity in the <u>total</u> life of the believer places the believer's soul in danger; therefore, since marriage is a part of the believer's <u>total</u> life, the absence of charity therein imperils the soul of either the husband or the wife, depending on which of the two is victimized.

In <u>The Doctrine and Discipline of Divorce</u>, Milton makes it emphatically clear that if one is taught to dismiss in general whatever hinders a spiritual state of mind, then the same rule must apply to the institution of marriage. If charity (love) is the fulfillment of the <u>whole</u> law, then charity must be the sovereign guide to Christian living. To test the spiritual value of a thing or being, one must measure it by the "rule of charity." If it does not measure up to the standard demands of charity, it fails the test and must be dismissed as impractical.

Matrimony was ordained by God for specific reasons which include various responsibilities on the part of each individual, and, in this case, especially the wife. Milton defines the nature of marriage and the responsibilities involved:

> For although God in the first ordaining of marriage, taught us to what end he did it, in words expresly implying the apt and cheerful conversation of man with woman, to comfort and refresh him against the evil of solitary life, not mentioning the purpose of generation till afterwards, as being but a secondary end in dignity, though not in necessitie; yet now, if any two be but once handed in the Church and have tasted in any sort of the nuptiall bed, let them finde themselves never so mistak'n in their dispositions through any error, concealment, or misadventure, that through their different tempers, thoughts, and constitutions, they can neither be to one another a remedy against loneliness, nor live in any union or contentment all their days, yet they shall, so they be but found suitably weapon'd to the lest possibilitie of sensuall enjoyment, be made, spight of <u>antipathy</u> to fadge together, and combine as they may to their unspeakable wearisomeness & despaire of all sociable delight in the ordinance which God establisht to that very end.[43]

In this passage, "cheerful conversation" indicates that there is mental union between the conversationalists. Charity must abide first in marriage, for it is charity that creates the atmosphere for "cheerful conversation." In Milton's language, a "fit mind" automatically signifies a "spiritual mind" which is heedful of the believer's first obligation. The wife's mantal capacity is vital because of her great capability of influencing her husband: she can encourage him either to love God or turn completely away from God. "Cheerful conversation" flows from a "fit mind," that mind which endeavors, at all times, to worship and praise God. In the divorce tracts, the mind is the instrument of charity and, therefore, the fitness of the mind determines whether or not an individual is capable of understanding his responsibilities first to his Creator and then to his fellow-man. The "fit mind" can distinguish between what does and what does not contribute to an atmosphere conducive of charity. When Milton continuously argues that the mind must be cared for first, he is really pleading the case of charity. The "fit wife" possesses a "fit mind" and she is aware of her place in marriage as subordinate to that of her husband. She recognizes herself as an aid to her husband's spiritual salvation, only because she honors the love of God. Otherwise, she would not be a "helpmeet" and would be sure to interfere with her husband's ability to commune with God.

A marriage without charity is sure to have internal unrest and unhappiness, and for a believer to be forced to remain in such a state of discontentment defies all that Christ taught man. An unhappy state of marriage destroys a man spiritually. Before one can concentrate on God, he must find peace within and without. Milton explains that

> nothing more then disturbance of minde
> suspends us from approaching to God.
> Such a disturbance especially as both
> assaults our faith and trust in Gods
> providence, and ends, if there be not
> a miracle of vertue on either side,
> not onely in bitterness and wrath, the
> canker of devotion, but in a desperate

and vitious carelesnes; when he sees himself
without fault of his train'd by a deceitfull
bait into a snare of misery, betrai'd by an
alluring ordinance, and then made the thrall
of heaviness & discomfort by an undivorcing
Law of God, as he erroneously thinks, but of
mans inequitie, as the truth is; for that
God preferres the free and cheerful worsiip
of a Christian, before the grievous and
exacted observance of an unhappy marriage,
besides that the generall maxims of Religion
assure us, will be more manifest by drawing
a paralel argument from the ground of divorcing an Idolatresse, which was, lest she
should alienate his heart from the true worship of God: and what difference is there
whether she pervert him by superstition by
[her] enticing sorcery, or disinable him in
the whole service of God through the disturbance of her unhelpful and unfit society,
and so drive him at last through mumuring
and despair to thoughts of Atheism: neither
doth it lessen the cause of separating, in
that the one willingly allures him from his
faith, the other perhaps unwillingly drives
him: for in the account of God it comes all
to one that the wife looses him a servant;
and therefore by all the united force of the
Decalogue she ought to be disbanded, unlesse
we must set mariage above God and charitie,
which is a doctrine of devils no lesse then
forbidding to marry.44

Without any doubt, Milton considers a man's earthly or temporal existence as a very important part of his spiritual existence. In the temporal society, the believer lives in anticipation of the kingdom of God. This is the essence of St. Augustine's lessons on charity. One must do nothing to hinder his successful return to his "native country"--Heaven. It is for this reason that St. Augustine explained the difference between "those things to be loved" and "those things to be used," and that Milton expounded the belief that divorce is a good thing when it fees a man from the bondage of an unhelpful marriage and sets him on a smoother path which leads to the kingdom of God. In the perspective of a husband, according to Milton, a wife must be loved as a useful means to a spiritual end, not as the ultimate end of all earthly endeavors. Milton supports this manner of thinking with a scriptural reference on the title page of the 1643 edition of <u>The Doctrine and Discipline of Divorce</u>: Matthew 13: 52, "Every Scribe instructed to the kingdom of Heav'n, is like the maister of a house which bringeth out of his treasure things old and new." If this verse is read in the context of the preceding parables of Christ, verses 44-50, one sees that what is most important in the temporal life is man's quest for the kingdom of God. In verses 45-46 (RSV), the kingdom of God is "like a merchant in search of fine pearls, who, on finding one pearl of great value, went and sold all that he had and bought it." After Christ had taught several parables of this kind, he ended with verse 52, wherein the scribe is compared with the master of a household. Milton considers himself as such a scribe, "trained for the kingdom of Heaven," who, like Christ, uses the old to clarify the new within the Scripture. Where Christ used an old everyday situation to describe the kingdom of God, Milton takes the old common denominator of Christian life--charity-- and gives it a new application which is, to him, its proper application. This verse also carries with it some symbolism of the Old and New Testament. It is Milton who sees the affinity between the two, both having the same end, "instruction" to the kingdom of God, even in matrimony. D. W. Robertson has reminded us that this basic relationship between the Old and the New Testament was seen by St. Augustine who felt that charity might be found in the Old Testament if one understands that "the writings therein embodied were also inspired by the Holy Spirit,"[45] the same Holy Spirit that is the giver of charity (love) in the New Testament and which is interpreted, by St. Augustine, as charity itself.

It is evident that, in the first divorce tract, charity is the most important of virtues. Charity guides man to all truth and to follow charity is to obey all of the commandments. If one follows charity in all that he does, his ultimate goal must be an inheritance of the kingdom of God and union with the Father. This end is far more important than marriage. As St. Augustine stressed, man's eternal end is what counts; and, as Milton believed, even in marriage, the journey toward the blessed should be man's daily preoccupation.

The controversy over the Mosaic law and the Gospel of Jesus Christ on the subject of marriage and divorce had to be settled before Milton could clearly argue his case. The two passages of scripture are Deuteronomy 24: 1 and Matthew 19: 3-9. The general consensus of Milton's contemporaries was that the Mosaic law, which stated that "'When a man hath tak'n a wife and married her, and it come to passe that she finde no favour in his eyes, because he hath found some uncleannesse in her, let him write her a bill of divorcement, and give it in her hand, and send her out of his house,'"[46] was abrogated by the words of Christ, "'Whosoever shall put away his wife, except it be for fornication, and shall marry another, committeth adultery.'"[47] William R. Parker states that

> The way in which it [divorce] was apparently managed under the law of Moses seems to Milton perfectly reasonable: the conscience of the husband could decide whether or not his wife, or he, or the both of them, felt hopelessly mismated. It is too intimate and subtle a matter to be tried by law, although the magistrate should see to it that the condition of the divorce is just and and equal. Milton could imagine no other way of protecting the wife from embarassment and integrity than to trust the husband to handle the business fairly.[48]

Milton does object to "the argument of those who interpret the law of Moses as only the premises [sic] of a succeeding law (as though God's people 'should be let to wallow in adulterous marriages almost two thousand years for want of a direct law'!)."[49] It is a fact that Christ's words to the Pharisees were to be taken as "a reproof" rather than "a command to posterity."[50]

The problem has been the interpretation of the Mosaic law, specifically the phrase "some uncleannesse." Milton interprets the phrase in terms of the mind:

> And what greater nakednes or unfitness of mind then that which hinders ever the solace and peaceful society of the maried

> couple, and what hinders that more than
> the unfitnes and defectivenes of an un-
> conjugal mind. The cause therefore of
> divorce expres't in the position cannot
> but agree with that describ'd in the best
> and equalest sense of Moses Law.[51]

To say that the Mosaic law was abrogated by the Gospel opposes the principles of Christ. The issue is a purely moral one:

> Which being a matter of pure charity,
> is plainly moral, and more now in
> force then ever: therefore surely
> lawfull. For if under the Law such
> was God's gracious indulgence, as
> not to suffer the ordinance of his
> goodnes and favour, through any error
> to be ser'd and stigmatiz'd upon his
> servants to their misery and thraldome,
> much lesse will he suffer it now under
> the covenant of grace, by abrogating his
> former grant of remedy and releef.[52]

The reason behind God's sanctioning of marriage, to remedy the loneliness of man, makes it ironical that God would permit man to remain in a situation where this end is not being accomplished, "without suffering charity to step in and doe a confest good work of parting those whom nothing holds together, but this of Gods joyning, falsly suppos'd against the expresse end of his own ordinance."[53] When God declared that man should not be alone, He did not think of sensual pleasure as the remedy of loneliness, but, rather, He thought of the mind. Where the body pleases but the mind is deficient, loneliness may still persist:

> And with all generous persons maried
> thus it is, that where the mind and
> person pleases aptly, there some un-
> accomplishment of the bodies delight
> may be better born with, then where
> the minde hangs off in an unclosing
> disproportion, though the body be as
> it ought; for there all corporall
> delight will soon become unsavoury and
> contemptible. And the solitariness of
> man, which God had namely and principal-
> ly ordered to prevent by mariage, hath

> no remedy, but lies under a worse con-
> dition then the loneliest single life;
> for in single life the absence and re-
> moteness of a helper might inure him to
> expect his own comforts out of himselfe,
> or to seek with hope; but here the contin-
> uall sight of his deluded thoughts without
> cure, must needs be to him, if especially
> his complexion incline him to melancholy,
> a daily trouble and paine of losse in
> some degree like that which Reprobates
> feel.[54]

To Milton--and to us--the mind is the most important area of concern in marriage. Canon law had not taken this into consideration, but, instead, regarded infidelity toward the body as a most abominable crime--not infidelity toward God. It is probable that the supporters of the Canon Law admitted to themselves that peace and love are the components of a happy marriage and that it is "the minde from whence must flow the acts of peace and love, a far more precious mixture then the quintessence of an excrement,"[55] but settled for a lesser practicality. Milton makes clear his belief that such willingness to follow tradition is "dishonorable to the undervalu'd soule of men, and even to Christian doctrine it self."[56] Emerging with Plato in the back of his mind, Milton relates that "all ingenuous men will see that the dignity & blessing of mariage is plac't rather in the mutual enjoyment of that which the wanting soul needfully seeks, then of that which the plenteous body would jollily give away."[57] This refers us to a passage from St. Augustine quoted earlier in chapter two. As for St. Augustine,

> intelligatur Legis et omnium divinarum
> Scripturarum plentitude et finis esse
> dilectio rei qua fruendum est, et rei
> quae nobiscum ea re frui potest (it is
> to be understood that the plentitude and
> end of the Law and of all the sacred
> Scriptures is the Love of a Being which
> is to be enjoyed and of a being that can
> share that enjoyment with us).[58]

Herein is the Augustinian doctrine of things (including men) to be used and things to be enjoyed. The wife, for Milton, is a thing to be used and enjoyed by the husband in his journey toward the blessed Creator and giver of love. There can be no sharing of the enjoyment of the love of God if one party does not love God. That which the soul needs most is salvation, and the spiritual journey should be a joyful and cheerful one. When there is an unfit mate, a man neglects his Christian duty: "doubtless his whole duty of serving God must needs be blurr'd and tainted with a sad unpreparednesse and dejection of spirit, wherein God has no delight."[59]

Man's good lies in spiritual contentment and an unhappy marriage is obviously contrary to this good:

> therefore to enjoyn the indissoluble keeping of a mariage found unfit against the good of man both soul and body, as hath been evidenc't, is to make an Idol of mariage, to advance it above the worship of God and the good of man, to make it a transcendent command, above both the second and the first Table, which is a most prodigious doctrine.[60]

If such a marriage continues, it means "the divorcing of God finally from such a place."[61] According to Milton, the good of man is whatever makes it more possible for him to reach his spiritual end. It was incredible, Milton thought, to think that the Law should have more mercy for man than the Gospel. In the Old Testament, under the Mosaic law, man could dissolve an "unfit" marriage. In the New Testament, without the "rule of charity," man could not dissolve an "unfit" marriage, but was forced to live in misery. Since the Old Testament and the New Testament provided differing perspectives on divorce, according to contemporary interpretation, Milton chose to analyze Christ's comments to the Pharisees.

The Pharisees reminded Christ that Moses permitted the Jews to divorce their wives in cases where there was a hardness of heart. According to Milton, Christ answered as he did, in the extreme, since the Pharisees were known to have gone to the extreme in divorcing their wives for the most trivial reasons. Milton clarifies the fact that God would never have granted any law that permitted evil such as this. The whole idea was to free the hated party from the possible cruelty of the other. Because men had not changed and were as weak in nature at the time when Milton argued this point as they were in the time of Moses, the same morality that Moses invoked remains under the Gospel, for the good of man:

> The Gospel is a covnant reveling grace, not commanding a new morality, but assuring justification by faith only, contented if we endeavour to square our moral duty by those wise and equal Mosaic rules, which were as perfect as strick and as unpardonable to the Jews as to us; otherwise the law were unjust, giving grace of pardon without the Gospel, or if it give allowance without pardon, it would be dissolute and deceitfull; saying in general, <u>do this and live</u>; and yet deceaving and damning with obscure and hollow permissions.[62]

Again

> this can be no new command, for the Gospel enjoyns no new morality, save only the infinit enlargement of charity, which in this respect is call'd the new commandment by St. John; as being the accomplishment of every command of perfection farther then it partakes of charity, which is <u>the bond of perfection</u>. Those commands therefore which compell us to self-cruelty above our strength, so hardly will help forward to perfection, that they hinder & set backward in all the common rudiments of Christianity.[63]

God, in the beginning, was cognizant of what was good for man, when He said "It is not good that man should be alone; I will make him a helper fit for him" (Genesis 2: 18, RSV). There was then no need for divorce, since God made a <u>fit</u> helper. Man needed woman to share the enjoyment of the journey toward God:

> And therefore even plain sense and equity, and, which is above them both, the all-interpreting voice of Charity, her self cries aloud that the primitive reason, this consulted promise of God <u>to make a meet help</u>, is the onely cause that gives authority to this command.[64]

The law that Moses granted was an act of mercy, for the good of the man who found himself married to an "unfit" woman.

For Milton, the Law of Moses introduced the subject of nature. Milton felt that divorce should be granted on the grounds that it is unnatural to force two people whose natures disagree to remain married--this is what he calls "forced cohabitation and a sinful act." It is only rational that "where nature is discover'd to have never joyn'd indeed, but vehemently seeks to part, it cannot be there conceav'd that God forbids it."[65]

The next point of interest is the idea that adultery is less of an offence in marriage than an "unfit mind." This coincides with Milton's belief that the body is of less importance in marriage than the mind. A wife's ability to communicate with her husband relates to the soul's need for a shared communion with God, which can only be fulfilled through the mind. Concerning adultery, Milton wrote:

> For this fault committed argues not alwaies a hatred either natural or incidental against whom it is committed; neither does it inferre a disability of all future helpfulnes, or loyalty, or loving agreement, being once past, and pardon'd where it can be pardon'd; but, that which naturally distasts, and <u>findes no favour in the eyes of</u> matrimony, can never be conceal'd, never appeas'd never intermitted, but proves a perpetual nullity of love and contentment, a solitude, and dead vacation of all acceptable conversation.[66]

The subject of adultery is presented as Milton introduces his explanation of the response of Jesus to the Pharisees' questions about divorce. Jesus spoke in rigid terms, restricting divorce privileges to cases wherein one party is found guilty of fornication; however, this restriction was not made because Jesus thought the body was more important than the spiritual self, but, rather, because of the laxity of the Pharisees who were known to divorce their spouses unjustly. The idea was to curb one extremity with another extremity.

The true believer is much disturbed by an unhappy marriage, one that does not fulfill spiritual needs because of some fault in one of the parties, for "no man knows hel like him who converses most in heav'n," and "there is none that can estimate the evil and affliction of a naturall hatred in matrimony, unlesse he have a soule gentle enough and spacious enough to contemplate what is true love."[67] True love flows from God and he who can contemplate such love is aware of his Creator and the spiritual journey in the temporal world.

Milton clearly believed that the Canon Law was unfair and that much of the suffering in an unfit marriage was inflicted upon mankind by mankind himself. Christ called men to liberty, not bondage; therefore, to restrict a man from divorcing an unfit wife except for fornication would be definitely an unjustified restriction. As we have observed, most of Milton's antagonists had agreed that it does often happen that a marriage fails because of internal problems. We know that there is agreement here because, otherwise, there would not have been a Canon Law and so many books written about how to choose a wife or a husband. Since a man or woman could not divorce his or her spouse except on grounds of fornication, or perhaps desertion, the only thing to do was to be sure about the person before marriage. It was obvious that all marital problems did not result from fornication or adultery, or sexual incompatibility. Milton takes St. Paul's comments on desertion in marriage as an additional reason for divorce, thereby emphasizing that there is a multiplicity of vital reasons for divorce, the most justifiable one being spiritual incompatibility.

> Now if it be plain that a Christian may
> be brought into unworthy <u>bondage</u>, and his
> religious <u>peace</u> not only interrupted now
> and then, but perpetually and finally
> hindered in wedlock by mis-yoking with
> a diversity of nature as well as of
> religion, the reasons of St. Paul can-
> not be made special to that one case of
> infidelity, but are of equal moment to a
> divorce wherever Christian liberty and
> peace are without fault equally obstruct-
> ed.68

Milton pleads the case of "good men":

> which condition, rather then a good man
> should fall into, a man useful in the
> service of God and mankind, Christ him-
> self hath taught us to dispence with
> the most sacred ordinances of his wor-
> ship; even for a bodily healing to dis-
> pence with that holy & speculative rest
> of Sabbath; much more then with the
> erroneous observance of an ill-knotted
> mariage for the sustaining of an over-
> charg'd faith and perseverance.69

This is what charity demands. The Christian has permission to "dispence with the most sacred ordinances" if they do not permit him to fulfill his charitable obligations to God and to his neighbor. The fault of the divorce laws, as Milton saw them, did not lie in the decrees of God, but, rather, in the "unjust laws" of mankind. It is God's will that good men find happiness and peace in Him. God could not have contradicted Himself in the Scripture, telling man at one time to love Him with his whole heart, soul, and mind, and, later, bind man to an unhappy situation which does not permit him to obey the original command.

In <u>The Doctrine and Discipline of Divorce</u>, Milton provided us with the central theological basis of his radical views on marriage and divorce. Charity is the sovereign rule in the Christian's life. Its "grand commission is to doe and to dispose over all the ordinances of God to men; that love & truth may advance each other to everlasting."[70] Milton ends this first divorce tract in full force: "God hath put all things under his own feet; but his Commandments he hath left all under the feet of charity."[71] One may safely conclude that

> The maddening thing about the reception of his [Milton's] book [The Doctrine and Discipline of Divorce] was the failure of anyone to offer a serious criticism or undertake a reply. The book was widely bought, but most readers seemed to have stopped with the title or the first few pages. They gossiped about it, they did discuss its argument.[72]

Tetrachordon

In a third tract, entitled Tetrachordon and published in 1645, Milton continued his argument in favor of divorce on spiritual grounds, again invoking charity. According to Arnold Williams, "the title, Tetrachordon, means literally 'four-stringed.' It was the common term for the primitive Greek scale of four tones."[73] In this tract, Milton discusses four passages of scripture which deal with divorce. From the title page of this tract, Milton lists the scriptures as follows: "Gen. 1. 27.28. compar'd and explain'd by Gen. 2. 18.23.24; Deut. 24. 1.2; Matth. 5. 31. 32. with Matt. 19. from the 3^d to the 11th; 1 Cor. 7. from the 10th to the 16th." One can be sure that

> Milton was convinced that far from involving contradictions, these four passages, rightly understood, made perfect harmony--like the four notes plucked from the strings of the Greek lyre, the tetrachordon. His task was, therefore, to demonstrate this harmony by a minute examination of each of the passages, discussing the original Hebrew or Greek, interpreting, comparing, anticipating objections, replying to faulty commentary, and elaborating with appeals to both reason and human experience. He never questions the verbal inspiration of Scripture, but he insists that knowledge of God's will is not for the literal-minded; the Christian must use common sense directed by charity and reinforced by scholarship.[74]

We shall observe that Milton seeks to show that there cannot possibly be any contradiction between the Old Testament and the New Testament on the subject of marriage and divorce, for God demanded charity from the beginning.

There are several points that Milton seeks to clarify in this third tract, the first of which has to do with the first marriage and the condition of man at the time. The failure to recognize the "rule of charity" in matrimony is also the failure to recognize the true dignity of man which was established by God in the beginning when He created man in His own image (Gen. 1: 27-28). Of course, when man disobeyed God, he lost some of his original dignity, but, through redemption in Christ, he regained his dignity. Thus, Christian liberty freed man from the bondage of human degradation and indignity. When the Canon Law bound man to an ill-mated marriage, it ignored the love that Christ had for man and Christ's infinite mercy toward man. Such love also serves as an example for man to follow in his relationship with his neighbor. In the words of Milton,

> All which being lost in Adam, was recover'd with gain by the merits of Christ. For albeit our first parent had lordship over sea, and land, and aire, yet there was a law without him, as a guard set over him. But Christ having cancell'd the hand writing of ordinances which was against us, Coloss. 2. 14, and interpreted the fulfilling of all through charity, hath in that respect set us over law, in the free custody of his love, and left us victorious under the guidance of his living Spirit, not under the dead letter; to follow that which most edifies, most aides and furders a religious life, makes us holiest and likest to his immortal Image, not that which makes us most conformable and captive to civill and subordinat precepts.[75]

Milton would have every Christian understand that the good of man is spiritual well-being, not temporal comforts which are unrelated to man's spiritual end. According to Milton, if one is spiritually content in marriage, he is physically content. The temporal life must yield to the spiritual life. Marriage is only a temporal state, and, therefore, must yield to spiritual guidance. This is Milton's reason for constantly reminding his readers that generation is not the prime end of marriage, but, rather, a secondary end. The simple fact that both St. Augustine and Milton convey is that charity must be placed above everything. It is, says Milton, charity that "makes us holiest and likest to his immortal Image." To be like God is to be able to love.

The good of man is love and peace. For a long time, historians and literary scholars have emphasized the traditional Renaissance interpretation of the good of man as whatever man chooses for himself, as opposed to the medieval concentration upon God as the center of attention in the life of man--a view that many find degrading to "thinking" man. There is some truth to this interpretation; however, the problem is in thinking that, during the Renaissance, man divorced himself completely from God and concentrated only upon his own personal desires, or that in the Middle Ages man thought of nothing but God. Milton looks at the new emphasis on man in the Renaissance in terms of the spiritual man. In this sense, the highest good for man is the ability to know where he should be headed in this temporal world, the place which prepares him for final union with God. The traditional interpretation of medieval man contradicts Christian liberty, for a man must not be forced to worship God. Instead, a man must be given the freedom of choice, with the realization that he has a responsibility to God and to his fellow-man.

Matrimony is a state of life that a man chooses in his temporal existence, but he chooses it in full recognition of his spiritual existence. Matrimony should aid a man in his communion with God, for this relationship should be of the same nature as that of Christ and the church.

> Moreover, if man be the image of God
> which consists in holines, and woman ought
> in the same respect to be the image and
> companion of man, in such wise to be lov'd,

> as the church, and Christ the head of man,
> so man is the head of woman; I cannot see
> by this golden dependence of headship and
> subjection, but that Piety and Religion is
> the main tye of Christian Matrimony: So
> as if there be found between the pair a
> notorious disparity either of wickedness or
> heresie, the husband by all manner of right
> is disingag'd from a creature, not made and
> inflicted on him to the vexation of his
> righteousness.[76]

For those who accuse Milton of misogyny, it is interesting to note that Milton gives the wife the same rights as the husband under the "rule of charity":

> the wife also, as her subjection is termi-
> nated in the Lord, being her self the
> redeem'd of Christ, is not still bound
> to be the vassal of him, who is the bond-
> slave of Satan: she being now neither
> image nor the glory of such a person, nor
> made for him, nor left in bondage to him;
> but hath recours to the wing of charity,
> and protection of the Church.[77]

The first priority in marriage is the love of God and the remembrance that God made man in His image.

Milton, in <u>Tetrachordon</u>, strengthens his argument for divorce by using the method of analogy to prove his point that the Gospel could not have contradicted the Mosaic Law and that charity is the end of both the Old Testament and the New Testament. He uses Genesis 2: 18, 23, 24, to explain Genesis 1: 27, 28. God's first concern was that man not be lonely, and, so, woman was created as man's companion, to be a "fit help, and, meet society." According to Milton, "all things that have bin nam'd were approv'd of God to be very good: loneliness is the first thing which Gods eye nam'd not good."[78] But, even with this statement, it is a mistake to think that the body rather than the mind eradicates loneliness:

> We man conclude therefore seeing orthodox-
> all Expositers confesse to our hands, that
> by lonelines is not only meant the want of

> copulation, and that man is not lesse
> alone my turning in a body to him, un-
> lesse there be within it a minde answer-
> able, that it is a work more worthy the
> care and consultation of God to provide
> for the worthiest part of man which is his
> minde, and not unnaturally to set it
> beneath the formalities and respects of the
> body, to make it a servant of its owne
> vassall, I say we may conclude that such
> a mariage, wherein the minde is so dis-
> grac't and villify'd below the bodies
> interest, and can have no just or toler-
> able contentment, is not of God's institu-
> tion, therefore no marriage.[79]

As we study Milton, it becomes most obvious that he was primarily concerned about the spiritual welfare of man just as St. Augustine was when he taught the doctrine of charity. We find that each marriage partner is a thing to be used, in Augustinian terms, in the attainment of the Beloved. Matrimony is an institution to be <u>used</u> for the good of both parties involved:

> And heer again, as before, I doe not
> require more full and faire deductions
> than the whole consent . . . our Divines
> usually raise from this text, that in
> matrimony there must be first a mutual
> help to piety, next to civill fellow-
> ship of love and amity, then to genera-
> tion, so to household affairs, lastly
> the remedy of incontinence.[80]

To think of matrimony in any other terms is to turn nature upside down and to ignore the spiritual needs of the mind.[81] When Adam said in verse 23 that "this is now bone of my bones, and flesh of my flesh," he was merely referring to the unity "of love and solace and meet help" that he was to find in Eve, not just the literal fact of creation.

When helpfulness, solace, and love disappear in a marriage, no longer is there a marriage. It is at this point that "the divine and softning breath of charity" steps in and "turns and windes the dictate of every positive command [that was given in the Gospel], and shapes it to the good of mankind."[82] Only love, solace, and helpfulness can make a marriage unified in one flesh. As in <u>The Doctrine and Discipline of Divorce</u>, Milton continues to propound the belief that the forcing of two ill-natured ones together is not only unnatural but in opposition to the "rule of charity." As man is the image of God, marriage is the image of Christ and the Church.

    Milton still finds it necessary, in <u>Tetrachordon</u>, to elaborate upon the problem verses of the Old Testament, Deuteronomy 24: 1, 2, "'When a man hath taken a wife, and married her, and it comes to pass that she find no favour in his eyes, because he hath found some uncleannes in her, then let him write her a bill of divorcement, and give it in her hand, and send her out of his house. (2) And when she is departed out of his house, she may goe and be another man's wife.'"[83] For Milton, this is law, and a righteous law. Milton gives eleven reasons for the existence of this law, which was not abrogated by Christ: 1) marriage cannot take place over the "dictates of nature"; 2) every ordinance must be for the "good and comfort of man"; 3) any covenant between man and man is binding only as long as it is "intended to the good of both parties"; 4) the Law did not "neglect men under greatest sufferances"; 5) the Law promoted "liberty and human dignity"; 6) divorce was permitted to release the husband or wife from undue sufferage; 7) the Law recognized the fact that "the power of marriage it self for its own peace and honour" may dissolve itself; 8) the Law permitted divorce for an innocent man whose wife has been deflowered; 9) the Law did not penalize a man for making a mistake in choice; 10) the Law recognized marriage as a symbol of the relationship between Christ and the Church; and 11) since marriage was one of the means of seeking "holy seed," the Law recognized the impossibility of accomplishing this end when there is an unfit marriage.[84] Milton has already explained the meaning of the word <u>uncleannes</u> to mean a number of things, including an unfit mind. Milton wishes to explain that in the beginning, when God ordained marriage, it was indissoluble only when the two natures were compatible and when the wife was a helpmeet to religion. Otherwise, God granted that an unfit woman should be divorced, according to Deuteronomy 24: 1.

One aspect of Milton's argument which surfaces over and over again is that God has endowed man with a nature which makes him knowledgeable of what is right for him, an endowment related to the spiritual segment of man. On this basis, it is irrational to force together two things (beings) who have nothing in common, except a body. Since the nature of man is to seek that which is best for him, and what is best for him is contentment in the hope of his spiritual end, then

> The general end of every Ordinance, of every severest, every divinest, even of Sabbath is the good of man, yea his temporal good not excluded. But marriage is one of the benignest ordinances of God to man, whereof both the general and particular end is the peace and contentment of man's mind, as the institution declares.[85]

The mind is placed in a category with the soul and "the Soul . . . excells the body," and "the body without the Soul is a meer senseles trunck."[86] For those who say that marriage is a covenant and therefore must not be dissolved, they must remember that there is a triangle of involvement here. God, to whom all reverence must be given in a marriage, witnesses the covenant between the couple of a marriage. But in the event that the two cannot live together happily because of an incompatibility of natures, God's having witnessed the marriage does not bind the couple to their covenant. The acts of witnessing and sanctioning are two different actions. It is rational to say that God witnesses every marriage, simply because He is omnipresent and omniscient, but it is fallacious to say that God sanctions every marriage. Milton believes that "forced cohabitation" not only affects a man's "service to God," but it indirectly affects the commonwealth.

A man's discontentedness makes it difficult for him to commune with God and to concern himself with the common good of his fellow-man. Certainly no law of God could command that one remain in this state of unrest. In this state of mind, one hates himself just as much as he does the one who causes his unhappiness. For this reason, Milton believed that divorce must be granted, not only because of natural incompatibility, but for the protection of the hated party: "The Law is to tender the liberty and human dignity of them that live under the Law, whether it bee the man's right above the woman, or the woman's just appeal against wrong, and servitude."[87] Nothing should disturb the spiritual contentedness of a man, for "Nothing more unhallows a man, more unprepares him to the service of God in any duty, then a habit of wrath and perturbation, arising from the importunity of troublous causes never absent."[88]

In the second part of <u>Tetrachordon</u>, Milton emphasizes, in more detail, Christ's responses to the Pharisees who asked Christ questions about divorce, reminding Him of the Mosaic Law. Milton teaches that Christ did not introduce any "new morality" or "new precept." In order to understand Christ's answer, one must realize something about the nature of the Pharisees in terms of what they thought of Christ. Christ's answers were based upon His knowledge of the motives of the Pharisees. Charity remains the "supreme decider of all controversie, and supreme resolver of all Scripture; not as the Pope determines for his owne tyranny, but as the Church ought to determine for its owne liberty."[89] As for the Pharisees,

> This law of divorce they had deprav'd both waies. First, by teaching that to give a bill of divorce was all the duty which the law requir'd, what ever the cause were. Next by running to divorce for any triviall, accidentall cause; whenas the law evidently stayes in the grave causes of naturall and immutable dislike.[90]

The New Testament statements on divorce must be read in the proper context. The one commandment in force in the New Testament, that which commands man to love God and his neighbor, encompasses the whole law of the Old Testament. The Mosaic Law was a moral law and so is charity a moral law, as marriage and divorce are matters of a moral nature. When Christ said that a man cannot divorce his wife except for adultery or fornication, He attempted not "to condemne all divorce, but all injury and violence in divorce."[91] Christ also knew that the Pharisees thought of marriage in a fleshly manner, and, so, He responded in that manner:

> And that our Savior taught them no better, but uses the most vulgar, most animal and corporal argument, to convince them, is first to shew us, that as through their licentious divorces, they made no more of marriage then be male and female, so he goes no higher in his confutation; deeming them unworthy to be talkt with in a higher straine, but to bee ty'd in marriage by the meer material cause thereof, since their owne license testify'd that nothing matrimonial was in their thought but to be male and female.[92]

Milton argued that Christ never forgot the chief ends of marriage to be spiritual and that when this is not achieved charity must step in and remedy the case. Christ's comments to the Pharisees' questions, then, did not condemn divorce when it is necessary for the spiritual health of one of the parties involved. Instead, Christ recognized the insincere motives of the Pharisees. The fact that no man must separate what God has joined remained true, but the conditioning phrase, "what God hath joyned," is also a determining phrase.

> But, heare the christian prudence lies to consider what God hath joyn'd; shall we say that God hath joyn'd error, fraud, unfitnesse, wrath, contention, perpetuall loneliness; perpetuall discord; whatever lust, or wine, or witchery, threate, or inticement, avarice, or ambition hath joyn'd together, faithfull with unfaithfull, christian with antichristian, hate with hate, or hate with love, shall we say this is Gods joyning?[93]

The simple fact is that God does not join every couple.

As the Pharisees would make God the creator of sin in terns of Moses' suffering divorce for hardness of heart, Milton continues to voice the conditions of Christ's responses. Christ never revealed to the Pharisees the other reasons for divorce. Milton sees the futility of such an argument offered by his contemporaries and combats the whole argument:

> How often shall I answer both from the institution of marriage, and from other general rules in Scripture, that this law of divorce hath many wise and charitable ends besides the being suffer'd for hardnes of heart; which is indeed no end, but an accident happning through the whole law; which gives to good men right, and to bad men who abuse right under false pretenses, gives only sufferance.[94]

Milton reiterates the truth that divorce was not necessary in the beginning:

> But from the beginning, that is to say, by the institution in Paradice it was not intended that matrimony should dissolve for every trivial cause as you Pharisees accustome. But that it was not thus suffer'd from the beginning ever since the race of men corrupted, & laws were made, he who will affirme, must have found out other antiquities then are yet known . . . . But after that the sons of men grew violent and injurious, it alter'd the lore of justice, and put the government of things into a new frame. While man and woman were both perfect each to other, there needed no divorce; but when they both degenerated to imperfection, & oft times grew to an intolerable evil each to other, then the law more justly did permitt the alienating of that evil which mistake made proper, then it did the appropriating of that good which Nature at first made common.[95]

Each of the New Testament references seem to be interpreted on the basis of the Pharisees' questions. Actually, Milton is saying that Christ purposely confused the Pharisees, but the Christian knows that Christ's words are best interpreted "by the unerring paraphrase of Christian love and Charity, which is the summe of all commands, and the perfection."[96]

Milton emphasized that divorce is a moral concern. In reference to Paul's teachings in I Corinthians 7: 10-11, "To be married, I give charge, not I but the Lord, that the wife should not separate from her husband (but if she does, let her remain single or else be reconciled to her husband)--and that the husband should not divorce his wife"(RSV), one gets the impression that Paul is against divorce. If one of the spouses is an infidel, Paul advises the Christian spouse not to resort to divorce if the infidel wishes to remain and change his or her ways. Milton points to a passage from Moses' Law in Exodus 34:16, and Deuteronomy 7:36, interpreted by Ezra and Nehemiah, which speaks otherwise: Moses' Law "commands to divorce an infidel not for the feare onely of a ceremonious defilement, but of an irreligious seducement, fear'd both in respect of the beleever himselfe, and of his children in danger to be perverted by misbeleeving parent . . ."[97] If the moral law of the Old Testament is an everlasting morality, not abolished by any new morality of Christ, then Paul's words, though accepted by tradition, are contradictory As for Milton, the Gospel verifies that

> not the law only, but the Gospel from
> the law, and from it selfe requires even
> in the same chapter, where divorce
> between them of one religion is so narrow-
> ly forbidd, rather then our christian love
> should come in danger of backsliding, to
> forsake all relations how neer so ever,
> and the wife expresly, with promise of
> a high reward, Mat. 19. And he who hates
> not father or mother, wife, or children
> hindring his christian cours, much more
> if they despise or assault it, cannot be
> a Disciple, Luke 14.

Again

> In mariage there ought not only to be a
> civil love, but such a love as Christ
> loves his Church; but where the religion
> is contrary without hope of conversation,
> there can be no love, no faith, no peace-
> full society, (they of the other opinion
> confess it) nay there ought not to be,
> furder then in expectation of gaining
> a soul.98

For one to remain with an irreligious person is immoral and, when he does, he remains at "the expence of all hopes."99 This statement should call our attention to St. Augustine's teachings that if one confuses those things that are to be enjoyed with those things that are to be used, he falters on the course that leads him toward the fulfillment of his hope--eternal communion with the Father.

Failure to divorce an infidel is a failure to remember the divine proclamation that man must love God above all things. The misconscruing of Paul's words in I Corinthians 7:12 is done from tradition, for Paul never intended men to believe that these words were from the Lord, but rather his own commentary. This, however, does not conclude the matter. How is Paul justified? The Law of the Old Testament condemned the dwelling together of Christian and infidel on ceremonial and moral grounds. The ceremonial law emphasized "the pollution that all Gentiles were to the Jews;"100 although "this the vision of Peter had abolisht, Acts 10. and clens'd all creatures to the use of a Christian."101 When Paul spoke the words of I Corinthians 7:12-13, he was speaking to the Corinthians who did not understand the cleansing of all creatures. If it should happen that a Christian man or woman finds himself or herself married to an unbeliever who wishes to remain and change, the Christian's duty is not to dismiss him or her but to try to convert this individual:

> Yet if a Christian full of grace and
> spiritual gifts finding the misbeliever
> not frowardly affected, fears not a
> seducing, but hopes rather a gaining, who
> sees not that this morall reason but
> better fulfill'd by the excellence of the
> Gospel working through charity.[102]

The case is different when the "infirme Christian" is involved. The attempt to convert the "misbeliever" incorporates Augustinian precepts which encourage the Christian to desire the salvation of another individual so that they may rejoice in the mutual love they share in Christ. It would be unjust to force an "infirme Christian" to remain married to an infidel, at the expense of losing his soul.

In <u>Tetrachordon</u>, Milton has attempted to strengthen his defense in favor of divorce by careful scriptural analysis, thus proving, as he set out to do in the first divorce tract, that when a wife fails to fulfill her obligation as a "thing to be used," she deserves to be divorced. He has repeated much of what he presented in <u>The Doctrine and Discipline of Divorce</u>, except there is more extensive elaboration upon the place of the woman in marriage and upon scriptural justification of divorce on grounds of spiritual incompatibility.

<u>De Doctrina Christiana</u>

In this later work, Milton said much the same thing about marriage and divorce that he said in the divorce tracts. There has been, however, some confusion about Milton's explanation of the Law and the Gospel in <u>De Doctrina Christiana</u>. Charity in both the Old Testament and in the New Testament, according to Milton, remains the spiritual guide of the believer. Milton explains:

> Therefore, as was said above, the end for
> which the law was instituted, namely the

> love of God and our neighbor, is by no
> means to be considered as abolished; it
> is the tablet of the law, so to speak,
> that is alone changed, its injunctions
> being now written by the Spirit in the
> hearts of believers with this difference,
> that in certain precepts the Spirit
> appears to be at variance with the letter,
> namely, whatever by departing from the
> letter we can more effectually consult
> the love of God and our neighbor. Thus
> Christ departed from the letter of the
> law, Mark ii. 27. "the sabbath was made
> for man, and not man for the sabbath,"
> if we compare his words with the fourth
> commandment, St. Paul did the same in
> declaring that a marriage with an unbeliever was not to be dissolved, contrary to the express injunction of the
> law; I Cor. vii. 12. "to the rest speak
> I, not the Lord." In the interpretation
> of these two commandments, of the sabbath
> and marriage, a regard to the law of
> love is declared to be better than a compliance with the whole written law, a
> rule which applies equally to every other
> instance. Matt. xxii. 37-40. "on these
> two commandments," namely, the love of
> God and our neighbor, "hang all the law
> and the prophets." Now neither of these
> is propounded in express terms among the
> ten commandments, the former occuring for
> the first time Deut. vi. 5. the latter,
> Lev. xix. 18. emphatically, not only the
> ten commandments, but the whole law and
> the prophets. Matt. vii. 12. "all things
> whatsoever ye would that men should do
> unto you, do ye even so to them; for this
> is the law and the prophets." Rom. xiii.
> 8. 10. "he that loveth another hath fulfilled in one word, even in this, Thou
> shalt love thy neighbor as thyself,"
> I Tim. 1. 5. "the end of the commandment
> is charity out of a pure heart, and of a
> good conscience, and, of faith unfeigned."
> If this is the end of the Mosaic Commandment, much more is it the end of the
> evangelic.[103]

In Book I, Chapter 10, of <u>De Doctrina Christiana</u>, Milton discusses marriage and divorce. His position is essentially the same as that in the divorce tracts. It may, however, appear that Milton alters the priorities of marriage from the mind to the procreation of children; but, if this is the case, the alteration is only a mild one and more a matter of interpretation. One must keep in mind that in <u>De Doctrina Christiana</u>, Milton deals with a universal Christian doctrine wherein some truths remain constant and are not changed. I think that Milton approached the scripture fully aware of the areas where compliance was in order. Of the ends of marriage, he said, "Marriage, therefore, is a most initmate connection of man with woman, ordained by God, for the purpose either of the procreation of children, or of the relief and solace of life."[104] The procreation of children, thus, is a purpose applied to marriage prior to the Fall. After the Fall, marriage was seemingly a remedy of incontinence.

Despite the purpose of marriage given above, Milton still believed that the sanctity of marriage does not provide for the lustful and beastly fulfillment of physical desire. Unless we accuse Milton of contradictions, we must justify his earlier comments on the end of marriage as the procreation of children. For genereations, the orthodox church taught man that coitus for any other reason (such as the fulfillment of fleshly desire) than the increase of holy seed for the kingdom of God was sinful. Hence, marriage for "the nuptial bed" and marriage for "the procreation of children" are two different ends. The former suggests the satisfying of the flesh, but the latter suggests a holy and righteous process ordained by God. As for what marriage meant after the Fall, it is worthwhile to mention that many of Milton's contemporaries spoke of two gifts from God to man: "the gift of continence," and "the call to marriage." The idea that marriage was instituted as a remedy of incontinence was only a recognition of a natural human phenomenon, and in no way diminished the priority of religion in the life of a married couple. In <u>Tetrachordon</u>, Milton stated that

> No mortal nature can endure either in
> the actions of Religion, or study of

> wisdome, without some slackning the cords
> of intense thought and labour;

and that,

> We cannot therefore alwayes be contemplative,
> or pragmaticall abroad, but have need of som
> delightfull intermisssions, wherin the en-
> larg'd soul may lean off a while her severe
> schooling; and like a glad youth in wandring
> vacancy, may keep her hollidaies to joy and
> harmles pastime: which as she cannot well
> doe without company, so in no company so well
> as where the different sexe in most resem-
> bling unlikenes, and most unlike resemblance
> cannot but please best and be pleas'd in the
> aptitude of that variety.[105]

These passages justify the necessity that a man have a fit companion, that is a wife who is able to communicate with her husband intelligently. She aids his spiritual being in many different ways.

Marriage should be built upon the love of God and one's neighbor. In the words of Milton, "The form of marriage consists in the mutual exercise of benevolence, love, help, and solace between the espoused parties, as the institution itself, or its definition, indicates."[106] Otherwise, a man is not required to continue such a relationship, one which God has not sanctioned. It should be obvious that God does not join such unions. In De Doctrina Christiana, Milton defines Christ's remarks to the Pharisees in the same manner as he did in The Doctrine and Discipline of Divorce and in Tetrachordon:

> The whole argument may be summed up in
> brief as follows. It is universally admitted
> that marriage may lawfully be dissolved, if
> the prime end and form of the institution be
> violated; which is generally alleged as the
> reason why Christ allowed divorce in cases of
> adultery only. But the prime end and form
> of marriage, as almost all acknowledge, is
> not the nuptial bed, but conjugal love, and

>mutual assistance through life; for that
>must be regarded as the prime end and form
>of a rite, which is alone specified in the
>original insitution. Mention is there made
>of the pleasures of society, which are incom-
>patible with the isolation consequent upon
>aversion, and conjugal assistance, which is
>afforded by love alone, not of the nuptial
>bed, or of the production of offspring,
>which may take place even without love:
>from whence it is evident that conjugal affec-
>tion is of more importance and higher excel-
>lence than the nuptial bed itself, and more
>worthy to be considered as the prime end and
>form of the institution.107

As in The Doctrine and Discipline of Divorce and in Tetrachordon, Milton does not say that the procreation of children is not an important part of marriage, but that conjugal love is more important. This seems right, for if there is no love between the husband and the wife, there can be no love for the offspring. Milton is consistent in De Doctrina Christiana, in that he continues to believe that the eternal moral law of Moses, which includes the edict on divorce, was not abrogated by the Gospel, but that the Ten Commandments written on tables of stone were abolished by the Gospel. No longer were they written on stone; instead, they were written in the heart of the believer by the Holy Spirit which taught men to follow charity, the fulfillment of the whole law, in all of their actions.

In this third chapter, the purpose has been to show the connection between John Milton's "rule of charity" and St. Augustine's concept of charity. It must be concluded that Milton, in The Doctrine and Discipline of Divorce and in Tetrachordon, emphasizes the importance of the mind over the flesh. In doing this, Milton was simply saying that a woman is unfit as a wife if she cannot hold a "fit conversation" with her husband. I have interpreted "fit conversation" to mean that conversation about religion, the love of God, and the love of one's neighbor. If this cannot be done by the wife, the husband's spiritual being perishes because of the lack of "fit" company with which to praise God. As St. Augustine taught that there are two kinds of things (those things to be loved and those things to be used), so did Milton believe in the difference between the two. For Milton, woman is "a thing to be used," her husband's helper and aid to salvation. Man, collectively speaking, is a thing to be used, a means to an end. When a man finds himself married to a woman who does not aid in this category, he finds liberty in the "rule of charity." It cannot be stressed too often that Milton believed that matrimony must not be cherished above God. He does not change his position in De Doctrina Christiana, but maintains that charity is the supreme guide and that spiritual satisfaction is superior to sensual satisfaction.

In the works of the traditionalists of the sixteenth and seventeenth centuries, one finds basic agreement in the fact that marriage, after vows have been taken, can become ungodly and disquieting. The only difference that one finds in the works of Milton is a position in favor of divorce: no one should be bound forever to an ungodly spouse and have his faith jeopardized. The "rule of charity" could, therefore, free man from such bondage and with scriptural sanction. Milton found it irrational to tell a man that he must remain married to a woman who interferes with his spiritual life, and, at the same time, tell him that his first responsibility is to keep his covenant with God. The intensity of Milton's beliefs can best be studied in two of his poetic masterpieces, Paradise Lost and Samson Agonistes, the basic concern in two of the remaining chapters.

IV

Marriage, Divorce and Reconciliation in Paradise Lost

> This extasy doth unperplex
>   We said, and tell us what we love:
> We see by this it was not sex,
>   We see we saw not what did move;
> But as all several souls contain
>   Mixture of things they know not what,
> Love these mix'd souls doth mix again
>   And makes both one, each this and that.
> --"The Extasy," John Donne

In the composition of Paradise Lost, Milton was able to strengthen, by exemplum, the argument that he had begun in the divorce tracts in favor of divorce. The delineation of Adam and Eve's marriage, in both the prelapsarian and the postlapsarian state, reenforces Milton's belief in the "rule of charity," rather than the Canon Law, as the determinant of whether or not a particular marriage must continue. In the marriage of Adam and Eve as Milton presents it in Paradise Lost, it becomes more obvious that Milton's interpretation of charity in relation to marriage has been influenced by St. Augustine's exegesis of caritas, from which emerges the doctrine of use. In reading Paradise Lost and concentrating upon the marriage of Adam and Eve, one must forever be conscious of St. Augustine's explanation of "those things to be loved" and "those things to be used," the former referring to the Father, the Son, and the Holy Spirit, and the latter referring to any earthly thing or being which serves as a means of reaching the Father, the Son, or the Holy Spirit, or of furthering one's salvation. As for Milton's application, attention is placed upon the woman as a "thing to be used."

While Eve, as Adam's wife, represents, in the prelapsarian state, the wife who is "fit" and able to further her husband's salvation, she most definitely represents, in the postlapsarian state, the wife who hinders her husband's salvation. In the two states, Milton depicts the harmonious marriage wherein charity is the key to harmony, and the inharmonious marriage wherein the absence of charity is the key to spiritual and marital failure. It is, however, in the reconciliation between Adam and Eve and in their spiritual reunion that Milton, for a second time, reenforces the message that charity leads to spiritual happiness in marriage and that without it physical satisfaction loses its virtue.

Suggesting that <u>Paradise Lost</u> is an exemplum of those precepts set forth in the divorce tracts, I shall elaborate upon the following points: 1) as a believer in charity, Milton automatically believed that the Christian believer's first obligation is to God, that one must love God above all things, including matrimony, as one progresses daily toward complete union with the Father 2) the marriage of Adam and Eve in the prelapsarian state is Milton example of what marriage was ordained to be from the beginning, a union wherein man and wife place God above themselves; 3) the marriage of Adam and Eve in the postlapsarian state, the first part of which represents divorce or separation of minds, is Milton's example of what marriage was not ordained to be from the beginning, a union wherein man and wife place themselves above God; 4) the period during which Adam and Eve are in confusion is Milton's chanc to show that a man's love of his wife above God is detrimental to his spiritual communion and that Adam might have saved his soul by refusing to accompany Eve in disobeying God; and 5) the progression toward reconciliation between themselves and with God teaches Adam and Eve that their sin has been one of disobedience--the sin of not loving God above all things--and that having achieved personal reconciliation, they, if they desire the reconciliation to be permanent, must learn well the lesson of charity.

I

There is no doubt that Milton believed in the general concept of charity, that all Christian believers must love God above all things. It is such belief that led him to question the refusal to apply the "rule of charity" to matrimony. There could not have been a more vital part of the Christian's earthly life than matrimony, a union founded by the Father. In the divorce tracts, Milton defends the believing man against the bondage of the Canon Law. In <u>Paradise Lost</u>, everything points toward Milton's insistence that charity must be honored first, that is, before matrimony. The man whom Milton defends must love God above all things before he enters matrimony; and, when he enters matrimony, he must continue to nurture his love for God, such love being cherished by a "fit" wife who also loves God above all things. God's plan for man was, from the beginning, that he become eternally unified with Him. The temporal scene before the fall and after the fall must be seen as a place of preparation for this eternal union with the Father. Before the fall, Adam and Eve are guaranteed eternal salvation, bypassing any physical death, if they will obey God as a sign of their love; after the fall and their spiritual reconciliation with God, they are promised eternal salvation through the grace of God, that is, if they remain reconciled to Him with unwavering love. Although they have a greater responsibility and will experience a physical death, they can find hope and comfort in the gracious promise of the Father. Their rule of life must be the "rule of charity."

That Milton believed that charity is central and that the Christian believer's first obligation is to God is evidenced in Raphael's lesson to Adam on the purpose of man's creation. In Book VII, Raphael reveals to Adam God's purpose in creating man. Satan, in his rebellion, had rejoiced in what he thought was the depopulation of Heaven. Satan did not know that Heaven retained "number sufficient to possess her Realms" and that his rebellion would have no lasting effect upon Heaven. Milton's God responds with definite measures:

> But lest his heart exalt him in the harm
> Already done, to have dispeopl'd Heav'n,
> My damage fondly deem'd, I can repair
> That detriment, if such it be to lose
> Self-lost, and in a moment will create
> Another world, out of one man a Race
> Of men innumerable, there to dwell,
> Not here, till by degrees of merit rais'd
> They open to themselves at length the way
> Up hither, under long obedience tri'd,

> And earth be chang'd to Heav'n, and Heav'n to Earth
> One kingdom, Joy and Union without end.[1]
>
> VII. 150-61

The significant words are those regarding man's present and temporal dwelling place--"there to dwell,/Not here, till by degrees of merit rais'd." In this sense, as St. Augustine stated in <u>De Doctrina Christiana</u>, life on earth is a journey toward the "eternal and immutable" and "if we wish to return to our native country where we can be blessed we must use this world and not enjoy it."[2] In the passage quoted, Milton implies that man progresses daily toward his "native country," which is Heaven. But he progresses only when he loves God enough to obey Him, that is, only when he loves God above all things.

Milton places words appropriate to his theme on the lips of the heavenly choir in praise of the created world:

> Witness this new-made World, another Heav'n
> From Heaven Gate not far, founded in view
> On the clear Hyaline, the Glossy sea;
> Of amplitude almost immense, with Stars
> Numerous, and every Star perhaps a World
> Of destin'd habitation; but thou know'st
> Their seasons: among these the seat of men,
> Earth with her nether Ocean circumfus'd,
> Their pleasant dwelling place. Thrice happy men,
> And sons of men, whom God hath thus advanc't,
> Created in his Image, there to dwell
> And worship him, and in reward to rule
> Over his Works, on Earth, in Sea, or Air,
> And multiply a Race of Worshippers
> Holy and just: thrice happy if they know
> Their happiness, and persevere upright.
>
> VII. 617-32.

Man's purpose on earth is to worship God first, and to bring forth more worshipers of God second. In the temporal setting of Eden, man has a relatively easy life--nothing actually changes from day to day. Man enjoys his existence because he daily fulfills his first obligation.

It will be noticed that Milton, in presenting the temporal scene before the fall, is true to scripture. He is consistent in believing that man's primary purpose on earth is to worship God in happy and joyful anticipation of his "advancement up" to the

Father. In presenting the temporal scene after the fall, Milton remains not only true to the scripture but also true to St. Augustine's exegesis of charity. Adam and Eve must leave Paradise, but they remain in a temporal world:

> They looking back, all th' Eastern side beheld
> Of Paradise, so late their happy seat,
> Wav'd over by the flaming Brand, the Gate
> With dreadful faces throng'd and fiery Arms:
> Some natural tears they dropped, but wip'd them soon,
> The world was all before them, where to choose
> Their place of rest, and Providence their guide:
> They hand in hand with wand'ring steps and slow,
> Through Eden took their solitary way.
> XII. 641-49

Perhaps the tears are "wip'd" immediately because there is hope as they remember the words of Michael:

> Yet doubt not but in Valley and in Plain
> God is as here, and will be found alike
> Present, and of his presence many a sign
> Still following thee, still compassing thee round
> With goodness and paternal Love, his Face
> Express, and of his steps the track divine.
> XI. 349-54

Adam and Eve have repented of their sins and, through the grace of God, have new hope. They

> may live . . . many days,
> Both in one Faith unanimous though sad,
> With cause for evils past, yet much more cheer'd
> With meditation on the happy end.
> XII. 602-5

The point that I seek to emphasize is that before and after the fall, there is the "rule of charity" that man must follow. The believer, as Adam and Eve are, must keep his eye on "the happy end," the reward of those who follow charity obediently. Charity entails obedience in the sense that if a man loves God before all things and in all things, then he trusts God enough to follow Him without question, realizing that man finds his spiritual and physical sufficiency in nothing other than God, his Creator.

It is very important that we understand the consistency of Milton's thinking regarding the general concept of charity, so that we will be able to understand the application of this concept to the specific case of marriage and divorce. There is no point in <u>Paradise Lost</u> at which Milton deemphasizes the first obligation of man--the love of God--the purpose of man's creation. Milton insists that when a believer marries, he must do so with full awareness that his relationship with God is to be nurtured in marriage. The wife or husband, as a "thing to be used," must aid the maintenance of this spiritual relationship with his or her fitness in spiritual things, an awareness of the Creator. Matrimony, in the temporal setting, then, must be subservient to the first cause of man's creation, the worship of God.

II

Milton's poetic characterization of the marriage of Adam and Eve in the prelapsarian state is built upon his own preconceived ideas of what a good marriage ought to be, as established by God and as Milton outlined them in the divorce tracts. Milton brings to <u>Paradise Lost</u> the same belief that charity must reign supreme in matrimony, just as it must in every other phase of Christian life. The doctrine of use which has been cited as a significant part of St. Augustine's exegesis of <u>caritas</u> is evident in the marriage of Adam and Eve. Eve recognizes her role as a "thing" to be used by her husband in his quest for eternal salvation. In creating the picture of a good marriage, Milton keeps in mind that "marriage is a human Society, and . . . all human society must proceed from the mind rather then the body"[3] and that the end of marriage is "the apt and cheerful conversation of man with woman, to comfort and refresh him against the evil of solitary life, not mentioning the purpose of generation till afterwards, as being but a secondary end in dignity, though not in necessitie."[4] Adam and Eve's marriage is indeed a "human Society" wherein there is "apt and cheerful conversation," all because there is a mental union which exists only because both Adam and Eve love God above all things, including themselves and their marriage.

Adam is aware of his first obligation to God and Eve knows that she must love God first, through Adam. She recognizes that she must be subject to and obedient to Adam, the express image of God. Adam and Eve are described as divinely created individuals:

> Two of far nobler shape erect and tall,
> Godlike erect, with native Honor clad
> In naked Majesty seem'd Lords of all,
> And worthy seem'd, for in their looks Divine
> The image of their glorious Maker shone,
> Truth, Wisdom, Sanctitude severe and pure,
> Severe, but in true filial freedom plac't:
> Whence true authority in men; though both
> Not equal, as their sex not equal seem'd;
> For contemplation hee and valor form'd
> For softness shee and sweet attractive Grace,
> Hee for God only, shee for God in him.
>   IV. 288-99

One learns much about the divine attributes of Adam and Eve from the narrator's description of what Satan sees as he surveys the Garden of Eden. Satan curses the sight, "O Hell! What do mine eyes with grief behold," for he sees in Adam and Eve what he himself has lost--"so lively shines/In them divine resemblance."

It is important for Milton to establish early in his poem that Adam and Eve are beautiful because they shine with "Truth, Wisdom, [and] Sanctitude severe and pure." They love the Lord with all their mind and soul. This image of spiritual affinity is the first that we get of Adam and Eve in the Garden of Eden, because spiritual unity is the first requirement of a happy marriage. Adam and Eve's marriage is harmonious because both are mentally unified and need each other as spiritual aids. Eve is created because Adam needs her:

>   how may I
> Adore thee, Author of this Universe,
> And all this good to man, for whose wellbeing
> So amply, and with hands so liberal
> Thou has provided all things: but with mee

> I see not who partakes. In solitude
> What happiness, who can enjoy alone,
> Or all enjoying, what contentment find?

Again,

> Among unequals what society
> Can sort, what harmony or true delight?
> VIII. 360-65; 384-85

In a state of solitude, Adam probably would have spent more time thinking of his loneliness than praising God. Eve is created as Adam's "fit help," a companion who is capable of sharing in the praise of God and His creation. In God's response to Adam's complaint, we learn that God never intended that man exist alone: He knew that this would not be good for man. This is one of Milton's points in the divorce tracts: marriage was first ordained as a remedy for loneliness. St. Augustine thought that salvation of the soul is best accomplished through another being, for whatever we love in another being must be the God that we see in the other individual. Adam asks his Creator, "how may I/Adore thee" without someone to share the joy? When Eve is created, Adam addresses her as

> Sole partner and sole part of all these joys,
> Dearer thyself than all; needs must the Power
> That made us, and for us this ample World
> Be infinitely good, and of his good
> As liberal and free as infinite
> That rais'd us from the dust and plac't us here
> In all this happiness.
> V. 411-17

And their responsibility is to

> ever praise him, and extol
> His bounty, following our delightful task
> To prune these growing Plants, and tend these Flow'rs,
> Which were it toilsome, yet with thee were sweet.
> IV. 436-39

Eve must enjoy God just as much as Adam does and trust the leadership of Adam:

> O Thou for whom
> And from whom I was form'd flesh of thy flesh,
> And without whom am to no end, my Guide
> And Head, what thou hast said is just and right.
> For wee to him indeed all praises owe,
> And daily thanks.
>   IV.   440-45

This conversation between Adam and Eve is "apt and cheerful," indicating an agreement of mind. Milton does not leave us with just a contract-signing ceremony; rather he shows us that this marriage will remain good and successful as long as charity is permitted to reign supreme.

The typical day in the life of Adam and Eve is one that begins with praises of God, passes with cheerful working in the Garden, and ends with praises to God. During the day, Adam and Eve are able to adore God through His magnificent creation. The typical morning hymn is filled with thankfulness:

> These are thy glorious works, Parent of good,
> Almighty, thine this universal Frame,
> Thus wondrous fair; thyself how wondrous then!
> Unspeakable, who sit'st above these Heavens
> To us invisible or dimly seen
> In these thy lowest works, yet these declare
> Thy goodness beyond thought, and Power Divine!
> Speak yee who best can tell, ye Sons of Light,
> Angels, for yee behold him, and with songs
> And choral symphonies, Day without Night
> Circle his Throne rejoicing, yee in Heav'n;
> On Earth join all ye Creatures to extol
> Him first, him last, him midst, and without end.
>   V.   153-65

Such words of praise continue for forty-three more lines. During the day, Eve works close beside Adam, never forgetting her relationship to Adam:

> My Author and Disposer, what thou bidd'st
> Unargu'd I obey; so God ordains,

> God is thy Law, thou mine: To know no more
> Is woman's happiest knowledge and her praise.
> With thee conversing I forget all time,
> All seasons and their change, all please alike.
>
> IV. 635-40

Milton works hard to explain why Adam and Eve's marriage is a happy one. It is primarily because of Eve's nature: she is a fit wife and conducive to charity in her husband. If we refer to The Doctrine and Discipline of Divorce, we will recall that an unfit wife, "through the disturbance of her unhelpful and unfit society," will eventually "disinable" her husband "in the whole service of God" and "drive him at last through murmuring and despair to thoughts of Atheism."[5] As for Milton, "nothing more then disturbance of minde suspends us from approaching to God. Such disturbance . . . assaults our faith and trust in Gods providence."[6] In this prelapsarian state, Eve's fitness is manifested in her willingness to obey Adam. She herself loves God and realizes that whatever she does can affect Adam's spiritual communion. Eve is then a useful instrument in the nurture of her husband's love of God above all things. It may be said that Adam and Eve's marriage is good because Eve obeys Adam and provides him with the peace of mind that makes him able to follow charity in all that he does. After the daily work in the Garden has been completed, Adam and Eve retire to their bower where they praise God together, "observing none, but adoration pure/Which God likes best."

Milton's portrayal of conjugal love teaches that such love is beautiful when it exists within the bounds of spiritual love. Beauty lies not in the satisfaction of the flesh but in the mental union which exists within the marriage. It is not until after we have seen Adam and Eve expressing their love for God that Milton draws our attention to the subject of the physical aspect of conjugal love. Within their bower, Adam and Eve

> Straight side by side were laid, nor turn'd I ween
> Adam from his fair Spouse, nor Eve the Rites
> Mysterious of connubial Love refus'd.
>
> IV. 741-3

In what might be called an aside, Milton says

> Whatever Hypocrites austerely talk
> Of purity and place and innocence,
> Defaming as impure what God declares
> Pure, and commends to some, leaves free to all.
> Our maker bids increase, who bids abstain
> But our Destroyer, foe to God and Man?
>   IV. 744-49

We must not forget that the choir of Heaven in Book VII (164) sings about one of man's secondary obligations, to "multiply a Race of Worshippers." Conjugal love exists within that marriage which is holy and happy because both parties love God above all things. The conjugal love that we see in Adam and Eve's marriage deserves the beautiful wedding song that Milton offers:

> Hail wedded Love, mysterious Law, true source
> Of human offspring, sole propriety
> In Paradise of all things common else.
> By thee adulterous lust was driven from men
> Among the bestial herds to range, by thee
> Founded in Reason, Loyal, Just, and Pure,
> Relations dear, and all the charities
> Of Father, Son, and Brother first were known.
> Far be it, that I should write thee sin or blame,
> Or think thee unbefitting holiest place,
> Perpetual Foundation of Domestic sweets,
> Whose bed is undefil'd and chaste pronounc't
> Present or past, as Saints and Patriarchs us'd.
>   IV. 750-62

It is obvious that Milton thinks that the conjugal love such as Adam and Eve exhibit is beautiful, and "where Love cannot be, there can be left of wedlock nothing, but the empty husk of an outward matrimony; as undelightful and unpleasing to God, as any kind of hypocrisy."[7] Conjugal love thrives on the first and most important kind of love--spiritual love. It is relevant, then, that Milton shows Adam and Eve first in light of their mental union in relation to God. It is here that Milton continues his plea that if the mind does not please, the body "will soon become unsavoury and contemptible."

    God rewards man with spiritual insight for his unwavering love of Him. The spiritual communion that Adam has with God is

verified by the angelic visits to him on earth; and Eve must be
given the credit for providing the peaceful atmosphere in which
Adam entertains divine thoughts and beings. The one angelic visit,
before the fall, is that of Rapael which covers Book V through
Book VIII. The purpose of Raphael's visit is to warn Adam against
faltering on his course. God's will is that the believer be
successful in attaining eternal salvation and this can only be
done by following the "rule of charity." As St. Augustine taught,
Adam, as a believer, must continuously keep his mind on his eternal
end, the arrival at his destined home. The end must not become
confused with the means. It is through continuous spiritual communion that man keeps himself abreast of his spiritual responsibility and guards himself against failure. Prior to Raphael's
visit, God has seen the need of rewarding Adam with this angelic
visit:

>   Them thus imploy'd beheld
> With pity Heav'n's high King, and to him call'd
> Raphael, the sociable Spirit, that deign'd
> To travel with Tobias, and secur'd
> His marriage with the seven-times-wedded Maid.
>   V. 219-23

Adam must be reminded "of his happy state," lest he "swerve not
too secure." Adam can only swerve through confusion of his end
with his means, and by forsaking charity in all that he does. Raphael reminds Adam of the one most important aspect of life:

>   one Almighty is, from whom
> All things proceed, and up to him return.
> If not deprav'd from good.
>   V. 470-2

To impress further upon Adam's mind the necessity of not "swerv-
ing" from the path that leads to God, Raphael recounts for him
Satan's rebellion and defeat, and the creation of the world and all
that dwell therein. Raphael's last admonition to Adam is

> Be strong, live happy, and love, but first of all
> Him whom to love is to obey, and keep
> His great command; take heed lest Passion sway
> The Judgment to do aught, which else free will
> Would not admit; thine and of all thy Sons
> The weal or woe in thee is plac't; beware.
> 							VIII. 633-38

Raphael warns Adam of what it means to be in happy communion with God. To avoid breaking this communion, Adam must remember that

> If we who enjoy and use things, being placed
> in the midst of things of both kinds, wish
> to enjoy those things which should be used,
> our course will be impeded and sometimes de-
> flected, so that we are retarded in obtain-
> ing those things which are to be enjoyed, or
> even prevented altogether, shackled by an in-
> ferior love.[8]

St. Augustine made it clear that the things which demand man's first love are "the Father, the Son, and the Holy Spirit." This is the end of man's spiritual endeavor. Everything outside of this spiritual love must be used toward the attainment of union with the Father. Raphael's lesson points toward Adam's possibility of becoming confused, thus giving up a superior love for an inferior love. This is noticed in Adam's speech about Eve:

> 					when I approach
> Her loveliness, so absolute she seems
> And in herself complete, so well to know
> Her own, that what she wills to do or say,
> Seems wisest, virtuousest, discreetest, best;
> All higher knowledge in her presence falls
> Degraded.
> 							VIII. 546-52

Adam uses the superlative to describe Eve, a description which seems more appropriate for the Father, the Son, and the Holy Spirit. Adam's confusion of end with means is indicated by the word "seems." The irony of Adam's rambling rhetoric is that what seems "wisest, virtuousest, discreetest, best" is not. Only God is. Raphael, "with contracted brow," sees Adam's weakness and cautions him to think of Eve in the proper perspective, a "thing to be used," a means, not an end:

> In loving thou dost well, in passion not,
> Wherein true love consists not; Love refines
> The thoughts, and heart energies, hath his seat
> In Reason, and is judicious, is the scale
> By which to heav'nly Love thou may'st ascend,
> Not sunk in carnal pleasure, for which cause
> Among the Beasts no Mate for thee was found.
> VIII. 588-94

Through Raphael, Milton has reemphasized the fact that man must not subject the "rule of charity" and religion to matrimony if he wishes to succeed in his progression toward total union with the Father. All indications are that this is the direction in which Adam is headed. Adam and Eve's marriage, so far, has been harmonious because they have been consistent in loving God above all things. Their marriage is guaranteed to continue harmoniously as long as each keeps the spiritual unity of mind. Adam must keep Eve in the right mental perspective, just as Eve must always be mindful of the role that she plays in the spiritual life of her husband.

III

From Book I to Book IX of <u>Paradise Lost</u>, Milton has given us the picture of a good and happy marriage. It is in Book IX that we begin to see the first signs of trouble in what has been a harmonious marriage: the signs of spiritual incompatibility, arising from mental disunion, begin to show. Just as Eve had been the reason for the happy marriage, because she understood her role as wife, she becomes the reason for the bad inharmonious marriage. In her desire to do as she pleases, she disavows her earlier commitments to God and to Adam. The typical day in the life of Adam and Eve changes. On the day of the fall, their day begins with the usual praise to God,

> forth come the human pair
> And joined their vocal Worship to the Choir
> of Creatures wanting voice,
> IX. 197-99

but it does not last throughout the day. On this particular morning, Eve does not address Adam as her "Author and Disposer" whom she will "Unargu'd . . . .obey." Eve has a will of her own.

    The most significant attribute of a wife, according to Milton, is her mind. The first error that Eve makes is in thinking that she can accomplish more separated from Adam. Such thinking indicates an unfit mind. Although Eve desires only to go to another part of the Garden to work alone, such separation represents more than just a temporal separation for a greater accomplishment, as Eve thinks:

> For while so near each other thus all day
> Our task we choose, what wonder if so near
> Looks intervene and smiles, or object new
> Casual discourse draw on, which intermits
> Our day's work brought to little, though begun
> Early, th' hour of Supper comes unearn'd.
> IX. 220-25

The thought of separation symbolizes mental disunion. Eve has begun to slip mentally. The whole beauty of their marriage has been Eve's willingness to stand beside Adam as a "fit" helpmeet, enjoying the beauty of God's creation with her husband. Adam has not forgotten Eve's importance in his quest for eternal salvation:

> Sole Eve, Associate sole, to me beyond
> Compare above all living Creatures dear,
> Well hast thou motion'd, well thy thoughts imploy'd
> How we may best fulfill the work which here
> God hath assign'd us, nor of me shalt pass
> Unpraised: for nothing lovelier can be found
> In Woman, than to study household good,
> And good works in her Husband to promote.
> Yet not so strictly hath our Lord impos'd
> Labor, as to debar us when we need
> Refreshment, whether food, or talk between,
> Food of the mind, or this sweet intercourse

> Of looks and smiles, for smiles from Reason flow,
> To brute deni'd, and are of Love the food,
> Love not the lowest end of human life.
>
> IX. 227-41

In one sense, Eve's idea is not such a bad one, for even Adam admits that "solitude sometimes is best society"; but, in marriage, the "human society" between man and wife is best. Adam and Eve's togetherness has represented a closeness to God, a union wherein the "rule of charity" is the guide. Whether or not Adam continues to love God above all things depends on whether or not Eve is there beside him to promote "good works" in him, that is to give him the peaceful and loving atmosphere necessary for communion with God. It is in Adam's uninterrupted spiritual communion that Eve was to have found salvation. The fact that Adam was "for God only" and Eve "for God in him" must not be taken lightly. It should be remembered that Milton, in the divorce tracts, talks specifically about the salvation of the husband. Adam cautions Eve:

> leave not the faithful side
> That gave thee being, still shades thee and protects.
> The Wife, where danger of dishonor lurks,
> Safest and seemliest by her Husband stays,
> Who guards her, or with her the worst endures.
>
> IX. 265-69

The heavenly messages were sent to Adam, not to Eve. Eve learns from Adam whatever she knows of God--except what she overhears.

When Eve refuses to subject her thinking to Adam's thinking, thus ignoring all that Adam has said regarding their happy state, free will, reason, and temptation, she indicates her unwillingness to be "used" by Adam in his attainment of spiritual union. She interrupts the mental and spiritual peacefulness of her husband. The happy marriage of Adam and Eve is dissolved the moment Eve "from her Husband's hand her hand/ . . . withdrew," and persisted in having her way. At this moment, Adam loses his peace of mind and, therefore, cannot love God with his <u>whole</u> heart, <u>whole</u> soul, and <u>whole</u> mind.

Through the sin of Eve and the compliance of Adam, Milton explicates a most important passage in <u>The Doctrine and Discipline of Divorce</u>, which has to do with the comparable evil influences of an infidel and an idolatress on their husbands. It is just as important to divorce an infidel as to divorce an idolatress because both will eventually lead their husbands away from God. When Eve returns to Adam after her fall, Adam forgets his end and considers the means. At the time when he should have shown his love for God to be greater than his love for his wife, he failed. The example serves to show to Milton's contemporaries who opposed divorce just what can happen to a man forced to remain married to an "unfit" spiritual companion. We must realize that the original Biblical story of Adam and Eve's marriage did not suggest that a marriage contract is binding regardless of any subsequent circumstances that might interfere with the spiritual harmony of the marriage, even though the story precedes the era of the Mosaic law of divorce in the Old Testament. In the beginning, the subject of divorce was not important because the marriage between Adam and Eve was created good and each individual of the marriage was given the freedom to obey God or not obey Him; and such freedom seems to me to indicate an inherent "rule of charity," which would not force any relationship, including marriage, to continue if it interferes with the continuance of a man's love for God. Milton understood this fact when he wrote the divorce tracts and when he chose this Biblical story of the first marriage as an exemplum of his precepts on marriage and divorce. The same "rule of charity" that holds marriages between believers together has the sovereign power to end such marriages wherein one party has subsequently become an infidel and thus has endangered the spiritual welfare of the believing party, in this case the husband.

Let us just assume that Adam typifies a man in seventeenth century England who sins because of divorce restrictions, even when his wife is not good for him spiritually. There are no doubts that Adam, at one time, loved God above his wife; but, at the same time when such love for God should have been exemplified as a sign of spiritual strength, Adam failed because of spiritual weakness. Adam, the "express image of God," sins because he has permitted his love for his wife to surpass his love for God. Milton's whole idea in the divorce tracts has been that if there can be no fruition of charity in a marriage, on the part of one individual, it is best that the marriage be dissolved by divorce to secure the spiritual welfare of the believing party. If divorce is not granted or desired, then matrimony becomes superior to charity and religion, a sign of disorder. Throughout the divorce tracts, Milton explains that man's complete happiness is found in the love of God. The first indication that charity is lacking appears when one finds his happiness in something outside of God. Eve's immediate thought after her fall is that she has found "full happiness":

>   shall I to him make known
> As yet my change, and give him to partake
> Full happiness with mee, or rather not,
> But keep the odds of knowledge in my power
> Without copartner?
>   IX. 817-21

According to St. Augustine, and as Milton agreed, "full happiness" can be found only in eternal communion with God, which results from a life in which charity reigns supreme. If Eve had remained the "fit" wife that Adam needed in his spiritual quest, her marriage might never have been flawed by sin. Just as Eve errs in thinking that all happiness is in her newly gained knowledge, Adam errs in thinking of Eve as the end, rather than the individual whom God created for him to be a means. Adam thinks that if he loses Eve, all is lost, not that if he loses God all is lost. Such wrong thinking leads him to resolve to die with Eve:

> How can I live without thee, how forgo
> Thy sweet Converse and Love so dearly join'd,
> To live again in these wild woods forlorn?
> Should God create another Eve, and I
> Another Rib afford, yet loss of thee

> Would never from my heart; no, no, I feel
> The link of Nature draw me: Flesh of Flesh,
> Bone of my Bone thou art, and from thy State
> Mine never shall be parted, bliss or woe.
> IX. 908-16

The language of Adam and Eve is now different and far from spiritual as it was before the fall. They speak only of themselves as they find happiness in the carnal or cupidinous love of each other. It is not God in each other that they love, but rather an inferior love of the body. Adam sees Eve in a new light:

> For never did thy Beauty since the day
> I saw thee first and wedded thee, adorn'd
> With all perfections, so enflame my sense
> With ardor to enjoy thee, fairer now
> Than ever, bounty of this virtuous Tree.
> IX. 1029-33

St. Augustine taught that "Those things which are to be enjoyed make us blessed," but Milton's Adam has never before been so enflamed "With ardor to enjoy" Eve. This is indication enough to assure us that Adam no longer loves God above his wife, that he has confused "the thing to be enjoyed" with "the thing to be used" in the attainment of the former.

We know that Milton capitalizes on the fact that Adam follows Eve in sin. This provided his contemporaries, many of whom were prominent divinity men, with a good picture of what they asked the believer to do in their persistent opposition of divorce--to deny God. There was no scripture that they could quote which indicates that God would sanction any law which causes a man to deny Him. Milton believed that in a marriage where one party loves God and the other does not, the "rule of charity" allows for divorce to guard against the endangering of the believer's soul. Therefore, it would have been to Adam's advantage to divorce Eve before the fall, rather than after his fall when he begins to realize the extent of his loss. The "rule of charity" would have been on his side.

Not long after Adam and Eve's "amorous play," divorce becomes an approaching reality, even if it is a delayed reaction on the part of Adam:

> Soon as the force of that fallacious Fruit,
> That with exhilarating vapor bland
> About their spirits had play'd, and inmost powers
> Made err, was now exhal'd, and grosser sleep
> Bred of unkindly fumes, with conscious dreams
> Encumber'd, now had left them, up they rose
> As from unrest, and each the other viewing,
> Soon found their Eyes op'n'd, and their minds
> Now dark'n'd.
> IX. 1046-54

Also, there

> Began to rise, high Passions, Anger, Hate,
> Mistrust, Suspiction, Discord, and shook sore
> Their inward State of Mind, calm Region once
> And full of Peace, now toss't and turbulent.
> IX. 1123-26

Adam grieves over his loss. He believes that if Eve had "heark'n'd" to his words, they would have "Remain'd happy." He also realizes that if he had refused to follow Eve, he might have "liv'd and joy'd immortal bliss." As Adam becomes more and more conscious of his sin, he hates the sight of Eve:

> Out of my sight, thou Serpent, that name best
> Befits thee with him leagu'd, thyself as false
> And hateful; nothing wants, but that thy shape,
> Like his, and color Serpentine may show
> Thy inward fraud, to warn all Creatures from thee
> Henceforth, lest that too heav'nly form, pretended
> To hellish falsehood, snare them. But for thee
> I had persisted happy, had not thy pride
> And wand'ring vanity, when least was safe,
> Rejected my forewarning.
> X. 867-76

In this scene between Adam and Eve, Milton is making a profound statement regarding divorce as Moses allowed it in the Old

Testament: that when a man fails to find favor in his wife, it is best that he "write her a bill of divorcement," give it to her and send her away lest such hatred lead to violence. Adam did not write Eve a "bill of divorcement" in black and white, but he certainly gave her one by word of mouth, which might have been just as effective as a written divorce.

The early episodes in the postlapsarian state clearly persuade one to believe that Milton is justified when, in the divorce tracts, he states that a marriage in which the love of God is absent is no marriage at all. In these early episodes, Adam and Eve have verified Milton's belief that the joy of the body exists only momentarily, but the joy of God lasts forever, or as long as one determines to love God above all things and people. Order in Adam's life became disorder when Adam chose to bask in the sun of what St. Augustine and Milton would call an "inferior love." By Adam and Eve's mistakes, one understands that God, when He blessed marriage in the beginning, never intended the institution of matrimony to be placed above the love of God, or charity. He intended that man and woman live in harmony of mind, always remembering, as Raphael taught, that "one Almighty is" and "first of all/Him whom to love is to obey, and keep/His great command."

IV

Throughout the scenes of accusation, Milton attempts to show that a man's love of his wife or matrimony above God is detrimental to his spiritual welfare, and, to avoid this, divorce would have been better. Such a belief is sanctioned by the Biblical "rule of charity," that man love God above all things, including his wife. Adam and Eve learn that their gain in knowledge is their spiritual loss:

> since our Eyes
> Op'n'd we find indeed, and find we know
> Both Good and Evil, Good lost, and Evil got,
> Bad Fruit of Knowledge, if this be to know,

> Which leaves us naked thus of Honor void,
> Of Innocence, of Faith, of Purity,
> Our wonted Ornaments, now soil'd and stain'd
> And in our Faces evident the signs
> Of foul concupiscence.
>
> IX. 1070-78

These are the words of Adam. His and Eve's shame over physical nakedness indicates a spiritual nakedness, a loss of those attributes which exemplified their love of God above all things. Adam and Eve's relationship with God has been "soil'd and stain'd." They have been stripped of their faith and purity, and the horror of it all is that Adam has made the wrong turn onto the path which leads away from God and Heaven.

One must see the importance and appropriateness of St. Augustine's doctrine of use as it is incorporated in Milton's "rule of charity." When Milton talked about the wife being a help meet, he had definite ideas in mind. The OED defines the word helpmeet as "a fitting or suitable helper, a helpmate: usually applied to a wife or husband." When one looks at the word as two separate words, one finds that the OED defines the word help as "anything or person that affords help; a source or means of assistance; an aid"; and the word meet is defined as that which is "suitable, fit, proper (for some purpose or occasion, expressed or implied)." From these definitions, one should be able to see the proper connection between St. Augustine's doctrine of use in the general application of charity and Milton's application to the specific case of matrimony. Adam was to see Eve as a "thing to be used" in his journey toward God. For Eve to be a helpmeet, she was not to concern herself with just the preparation of the meals and the making of the beds, but rather she was to concern herself first with nurturing her husband's spiritual life by loving the God that her husband loved and by comprehending this God in Adam. The cause of the fall lies principally in the unfitness of Eve and Adam's inability to detect this and do something about it. Since Eve was created by God, Adam's detection of any unfitness in her does not imply that God's creation was in any way imperfect

Any unfitness of Eve must be understood as Eve's own doing and not God's.

The doctrine of use in the concept of charity is the basic motif that runs throughout the divorce tracts. When a man's wife can no longer aid him in spiritual things, divorce is biblically sound, based on the doctrine of charity. As the believer must love God above all things, he must care for his soul before his body. In _Paradise_ _Lost_, Milton accomplishes much in the line of defending divorce according to Scripture. Even in a marriage between believers, as Adam and Eve were in the beginning, things can go wrong. How safe Adam would have been had he divorced Eve the moment she withdrew her hand from him and departed on her way to another part of the Garden! He might have been lonely physically but he would have been content spiritually. To continue a spiritually inharmonious marriage is, for Milton, unethical, immoral, unnatural, and, most of all, unbiblical. The new commandment of love in the New Testament could not have opposed the spiritual liberty of a man in pursuit of charity and eternal salvation.

Adam's problem has been that he came to his spiritual senses too late. The argument that he has with Eve after the initial joys of the fall wear off carries with it a consciousness that Adam should have possessed, if not at the sign of Eve's separation of mind, then certainly at her appearance after the fall. As Adam comes to reckon with his broken relationship with God, the pain and suffering of the man who loves his wife above God becomes an experienced reality.

V

The "rule of charity" is indeed a matter of prime importance in _Paradise_ _Lost_, just as it was in the divorce tracts. As Milton used the period following the fall of Adam and Eve to re-emphasize the urgency of divorce privileges to protect the spiritual welfare of the believing husband who loves God above all things, he uses the period following the fall, the period of reconciliation, to re-emphasize his belief that for a marriage to remain spiritually and physically unified, both parties must continue to love God above all things, including their marriage. This is their only means of staying on the path that leads toward Heaven. Adam must be made to understand that Eve was created to serve her husband as a "thing to be used," not to be enjoyed, lest he err in thinking that his spiritual end and ultimate happiness are found in his wife, rather than in God.

The lesson of charity begins with Adam's own recognition of his spiritual loss. Had he not transgressed, he "might have liv'd and joy'd immortal bliss." God's first cause in the creation was that a human creature worship Him and "by degrees" progress toward Him. The temporal world was to be a place of preparation, where man, though perfect in his station, might continue to improve until he reached the spiritual perfection that God would have him reach. Marriage was instituted as a temporal state within a temporal world, subject to man's primary spiritual duty of loving God first. God's plan for Adam and Eve was ideal. Mary Ann Radzinowicz describes it in the following words:

> Simply by the actions involved in voluntary obedience, Adam and Eve would perfect themselves, as though the steps to heaven were not fixed but moving, so that to stand would be to ascend. They were to better themselves in love so they would ascend the scale of heavenly love, were to improve themselves in diet so that their very bodies would take on more spiritual qualities, were to better themselves in the acts of fellowship that at will they could participate with angels and dwell either in Eden or Heaven.[9]

Eve, the unfit wife, brought spiritual calamity to what had been known as a happy marriage. Through inference, it is clearly stated in Paradise Lost that an iniquitous wife may bring damnation to the soul of her husband, and marriage is not worth the soul of a man. To Milton, it was incredible that such a common and fundamental Christian precept could not be understood by his contemporaries, that they would not accept the "rule of charity" as just as powerful and operative in marriage as it was given to be in other areas of the Christian life. How could Christ have abolished the Mosaic doctrine of divorce when He taught men to love God above all things and when He was the embodiment of eternal love? It is in the last two books of <u>Paradise Lost</u> that Milton closes the seeming gap between the Old and the New Testament, that is regarding charity in matrimony.[10] Adam is taught a perspective of love which encompasses the doctrine of charity in the Old Testament and in the New Testament. Everything outside of God must be used as a means of spiritual attainment, and, unless Adam can see his reclaimed Eve in this light, there is the danger of another catastrophe.

When God sent his "Vicegerent" to reprimand Adam and Eve, the first discovery is that Adam and Eve have lost something:

> Love was not in thir looks, either to God
> Or to each other, but apparent guilt
> And shame, and perturbation, and despair,
> Anger, and obstinacy, and hate, and guile.
>   X. 111-14

Without love for God and for each other, Adam and Eve could not succeed. Again, the loss of spiritual love, as a result of Adam's and Eve's choice of an ephemeral inferior love, shows that, even in reconciliation, the lesson of charity must be well learned before charity can be enforced. Christ's reprimand of Adam after the fall indicates Adam's confusion of Eve with God:

> Was shee thy God, that her thou didst obey
> Before her voice, or was shee made thy guide,
> Superior, or but equal, that to her
> Thou didst resign thy Manhood, and the Place
> Wherein God set thee above her made of thee,
> And for thee, whose perfection far excell'd
> Hers in all real dignity: Adorn'd
> She was indeed, and lovely to attract
> Thy Love, not thy subjection, and her Gifts
> Were such as under Government well seem'd.
>   X. 145-54

As Stella P. Revard has pointed out, Eve was not made incomplete. She was created with the mental equipment to understand "the requirements of her condition, the necessity of maintaining loyalty as the link with God."[11] Obedience to God rather than to Eve would have been a sign of Adam's love of God above Eve; and Eve's obedience to Adam would have been not only a sign of her willingness to be a "thing to be used" in Adam's attainment of salvation but also a sign of her unwavering love for God in Adam. Disobedience of God by Adam and Eve indicated that the lesson of charity had not been learned well, that Adam and Eve had not learned that "service to God must be voluntary, the effect of love, not of necessity, if it is to be acceptable."[12] C. S. Lewis pointed out that

> If conjugal love were the highest value in Adam's world, then of course his resolve would have been the correct one. But if there are other things that have an even higher claim on a man, if the Universe is imagined to be such that, when the pinch comes, a man ought to reject wife and mother and his own life also, then the case is altered.[13]

We can be sure that one of the inherent questions that Milton asks regarding the reconciliation is, will Eve be a fit instrument again, capable of aiding Adam's salvation? Eve's suggestion of suicide as a means of avoiding the guilt of bringing into the world a sinful race of men is evidence of her sincere sorrow for her past sin. Of course, Adam does not accept this suggestion because he has hope that God will forgive them and that there will be a better way. He says:

> How much more if we pray him, will his ear
> Be open, and his heart to piety incline,
> And teach us further . . .
> And what may else be remedy or cure
> To evils which our own misdeeds have wrought,
> Hee will instruct us praying, and of Grace
> Beseeching him, so as we need not fear
> To pass commodiously this life, sustain'd
> By him with many comforts, till we end
> In dust, our final rest, and native home.[14]
>
> X. 1060-2; 1079-85

If Adam and Eve are really sorry for their sins, it is probable that God "will relent and turn from His despleasure."

When Adam and Eve become reconciled to God, their marriage is reclaimed. Eve is willing to follow Adam and when a woman is willing to follow her husband in religion, she is classified as a "fit" wife. Togetherness in religion means a togetherness in mind, and, of course, for Milton, the mind is of major importance. In the prelapsarian state, Adam and Eve followed charity in all of their actions and they must continue to do so, now that they, in the postlapsarian state, are reconciled with God. Their reconciliation has come through Christ who presented to the Father their prayer that they might proceed "To better life" where the "redeem'd may dwell in joy and bliss." But, even with the reconciliation to God, Adam must remember that all amounts to nothing if he makes the same mistake again; and, for this reason, the archangel Michael is sent to teach Adam this truth, while Eve sleeps and dreams of spiritual things regarding the future.

The vision of the world to come that Adam has in Book XI has often been interpreted as a lesson concerning death, but it can also be interpreted as Michael's lesson to Adam on the "rule of charity" in Adam's reclaimed marriage. We must realize that Adam is the first character in an historical drama and that he has to be ministered to in a special way. As far as examples of persons exhibiting Christian integrity and of persons not exhibiting Christian integrity, there are very few for Adam to follow. The most outstanding models have been Abdiel and Lucifer, beings from a different world than the one in which Adam lives. Adam will benefit by seeing examples of both kinds of men in the world which he knows. As Mary Ann Radzinowicz states,

> Adam goes down into the world as a Christian, in his lifetime having been vouchsafed a foreknowledge of the redeemer, for Christ's redemption reopens action, makes courage, piety, and self-sacrifice meaningful. Michael comes to tell Adam what will be done throughout history in order that Adam can conduct himself as a Christian to embody as well as inherit Christ's kingdom.[15]

Among the examples given, Adam must desire to follow the example of those men who will be followers of charity in all that they do and are, therefore, successful in their attainment of "Christ's kingdom."

All that Adam sees and learns is related in some way to the lesson of charity, the love of God above all things, including Eve. The first lesson is presented in the story of Cain and Abel. Cain is typical man who does not love God above himself; he brings to God his second best while Abel brings his best. Abel dies a physical death but he gains an eternal life with God. The second lesson is presented in the story of the "Lazar-house." Adam learns about the true nature of temperance. Those who suffer in the "Lazar-house" are suffering because of their intemperance. As a result, disease has affected the body. The believer often shows his love for God by denying himself something. Intemperance or excessiveness symbolizes selfishness, such that does not permit one to love God above self. When these men forsook the image and love of God in themselves, "Thir Maker's Image . . ./Forsook them." The love of food above God has brought destruction, physical as well as spiritual. Michael's comment to Adam is "Nor love thy Life, nor hate; but what thou liv'st/Live well." He who lives well does so because he follows the "rule of charity." The third lesson is presented in the picture of the artists who fail to recognize their insufficiency without God (610-12). The fourth lesson pictures "Just men" who "all thir study bent/To worship God aright" (577-81) but forsook their study for "A Bevy of fair women" who lead them away from God. Marriages result, but Adam misunderstands what he sees:

> True opener of mine eyes, prime Angel blest,
> Much better seems this Vision, and more hope
> Of peaceful days portends, then those two past;
> Those were of hate and death, or pain much worse.
> Here Nature seems fulfill'd in her ends.
> XI. 598-608

Such misunderstanding shows the necessity of these lessons for

Adam. He must learn not to "Judge . . . what is best/By pleasure." Adam was created "to nobler end/Holy and pure, conformity divine." Michael explains what Adam has misunderstood in no uncertain terms:

> For that female Troop thou saw'st that seem'd
> Of Goddesses, so blithe, so smooth, so gay,
> Yet empty of all good wherein consists
> Woman's domestic honor and chief praise;
> Bred only and completed to the taste
> Of lustful appetence, to sing, to dance,
> To dress, and troll the Tongue, and roll the Eye.
> To these that sober Race of men, whose lives
> Religious titl'd them the Sons of God,
> Shall yield up all their virtue, all thir fame
> Ignobly, to the trains and to the smiles
> Of these fair Atheists, and now swim in joy,
> (Erelong to swim at large) and laugh; for which
> The world erelong a world of tears must weep.
> XI. 614-27

Adam's response to these lines is most important in the philosophies of St. Augustine and Milton. The sight is a sad one:

> O pity and shame, that they who to live well
> Enter'd so fair, should turn aside to tread
> Paths indirect, or in the mid way faint.
> X. 621-31

This is the essence of what St. Augustine taught, that man must not become confused in his journey toward the blessed; he must be able to distinguish between the means and the end. Milton, in his fight for divorce, on grounds of charity, felt that it was a sad predicament for the man who must place his soul in jeopardy because he has to remain bound to an iniquitous woman.

Milton argued in his divorce tracts that to inhibit a man from divorcing an unfit wife is against nature, a point which is illustrated in the fourth lesson of the vision. The result of the ill-mated marriages is unnatural births:

> Of those ill-mated Marriages thou saw'st;
> Where good with bad were matcht, who of themselves

> Abhor to join; and by imprudence mixt,
> Produce prodigious Births of body and mind.
> XI. 684-87

These afflicted children become the warriors against the just. By portraying the negative result, Milton is able to show such unhappy consequences, so proving the immorality of "forced cohabitation." Charity is still the theme: the just man is he who follows charity, whatever the cost, because he is sure of his salvation in the end. Of the one just man among these warriors, Milton says

> Him the most High
> Rapt in a balmy cloud with winged studs
> Did, as thou saw'st, receive, to walk with God
> High in Salvation and the Climes of bliss
> Exempt from Death; to show thee what reward
> Awards the good, the rest what punishment.
> XI. 705-10

The fifth and last lesson is presented in the picture of Noah In Noah, Milton shows another just man who followed charity:

> One Man except, the only Son of light
> In a dark Age, against example good,
> Against allurement, custom, and a World
> Offended; fearless of reproach and scorn,
> Of violence, hee of thir wicked ways
> Shall them admonish, and befor them set
> The paths of righteousness.
> XI. 808-14

Noah and his family are saved from the flood because he obeyed and loved God enough to believe in His prediction for the future, not being swayed by other things or people.

The entire vision helps Adam recall his first mistake: not loving God above his wife. Every man who fails to follow charity errs on the path which leads to Heaven. In each lesson of the vision, those who failed were those who thought of themselves above God. When Adam sinned, he sinned because he thought of himself first, not being able to imagine himself without Eve. Michael, in the vision, has given Adam a variety of pictorial examples which should be helpful to Adam in the future. If Adam is to start a new life in God, he must remember not to make the same error again: he must not find his ultimate happiness in something outside of God.

In Book XII of <u>Paradise Lost</u>, where Adam continues to learn of new hope in the prophecy of Christ's coming, Milton closes the gap between the Old Testament and the New Testament by indicating that man is still required to love God above all things, in both testaments. Of Christ's work on earth, Milton places specific words in the mouth of Michael. Christ will not battle with Satan physically:

> But by fulfilling that which thou didst want,
> Obedience to the Law of God, impos'd
> On penalty of death, and suffering death,
> The penalty to thy transgression due,
> And due to theirs which out of thine will grow:
> So only can high Justice rest appaid.
> The Law of God exact he shall fulfil
> Both by obedience and by love, though love
> Alone fulfill the Law.
>   XII. 396-404

Again, obedience is the sign of love. At the end of Adam's visit with Michael, Adam has learned

>   that to obey is best
> And love with fear the only God, to walk
> As in his presence, ever to observe
> His providence, and on him sole depend.
>   XII. 561-64

Michael's final words of advice to Adam are:

>   only add
> Deeds to thy knowledge answerable, add Faith,
> Add Virtue, Patience, Temperance, add Love,
> By name to come call'd Charity, the soul
> Of all the rest: then wilt thou not be loath
> To leave this Paradise, but shalt possess
> A paradise within thee, happier far.
>   XII. 581-87

Adam has learned that "Love itself is heavenly and the choices and decisions made in it are a profound part of man's salvation."[16] Adam returns to Eve who has been asleep but, at the same time, aware of the great future. Having reconciled herself with God, Eve sees Adam again as "All things under Heav'n." They are united in "one Faith" as they leave Paradise "hand in hand."

In *Paradise Lost*, Milton has defended his position on divorce most convincingly. Moving from the positive aspects of marriage to the negative and back to the positive, Milton has given us a composite summary of his defense of divorce. At the end of *Paradise Lost*, we are sure that Adam has learned that he must see Eve as a "thing to be used" in his attainment of eternal salvation and that matrimony is to be secondary to charity, as matrimony is a state of human existence within the temporal setting, governed by the "rule of charity." Eve has learned that her salvation is in Adam and that marriage is a "human Society" in which the ends are "the apt and cheerful conversation of man with woman."

V

Divorce in Samson Agonistes

> What'er it be, to wisest men and best
> Seeming at first all heaven'ly under virgin veil,
> Soft, modest, meek, demure,
> Once joined, the contrary she proves, a thorn
> Intestine, far within defensive arms
> A cleaving mischief, in his way to virtue
> Adverse and turbulent.

In these lines (1034-40) from Samson Agonistes, Milton reaffirms his position on the urgency of granting divorce privileges to the man who finds himself married to a woman who hinders, rather than aids, his salvation. One hears the echo of those words uttered in The Doctrine and Discipline of Divorce: "for all the warinesse . . .us'd, it may yet befall a discreet man to be mistak'n in his choice," for "who knows not that the bashful mutenes of a virgin may oft-time hide all the unliveliness & naturall sloth which is really unfit for conversation."[1] No book had yet been written by human hands that, if read carefully and followed strictly, could guarantee the avoidance of a bad choice in marriage and therefore alleviate the necessity of having a law permitting divorce. From the lips of Milton's Chorus come the words:

> Tax not divine disposal; wisest men
> Have err'd, and by bad women been deceiv'd;
> And shall again, pretend they ne'er so wise.[2]

The only hope of the believer who found himself in such a marital predicament was the "rule of charity" which gives the believer freedom to break any relationship which interferes with the love of God. As in Paradise Lost, so the emphasis in Samson Agonistes falls on the "rule of charity" as it is interpreted to be the "supreme decider" of divorce. The whole of Samson Agonistes deals with a husband's progression toward spiritual accomplishment after he has justifiably divorced his spiritually incompatible wife, the justification of which is given through flashbacks. Samson's marriage to Dalila provided Milton with the right example of all that he had tried to explain in the divorce tracts regarding the justification of divorce in that marriage where the husband's love of God is not being nurtured because of the annoyance of an unbelieving wife, a thing "unfit" to be used by a believing husband. Milton held that the believing husband had to be always mindful of his first obligation to God, the epitome of love, immutable love, in his quest for eternal salvation; and be able to enter matrimony with the understanding that his wife must be seen in the proper perspective in relation to God.

In view of the fact that Milton, in his divorce tracts, speaks in defense of the believer--the saint--who makes a bad choice in marriage, it is necessary, before we begin our discussion of <u>Samson Agonistes</u> as a poetic exemplum of those precepts presented in the divorce tracts, to understand Milton's choice of Samson as such a saint. As in <u>Paradise Lost</u>, Milton has chosen a well-known Biblical story, based on Judges 13-16; but, if one sees Milton's Samson as the Biblical Samson, he might consider Samson a bad choice from the beginning.

According to Judges 13:7 (RSV), the angel that appeared to Samson's mother, before his birth, announced that Samson would be the chosen of God, "a Nazarite from birth to the day of his death." As recorded in Numbers 6, a Nazarite is one who has separated himself to God and "all the days of his separation he is holy to the Lord." The symbol of his sanctification is his long hair upon which "no razor" must "come . . . until the time is completed for which he separates himself to the Lord." Obviously Samson did not choose to be holy and separated to the Lord; therefore, certain contradicitons are noticeable in his life: as one chosen by God, Samson marries a Philistine woman, of Timnah, has an affair with a Philistine harlot, and takes another Philistine woman as his mistress. Except for the first action which is prompted by the Spirit of God for strategic purposes, each of Samson's actions is wrong. In a footnote to Judges 16: 17, in the Revised Standard Version of the Bible, edited by Hubert G. May and Bruce M. Metzger, it is stated that "the story that

Samson was a Nazarite (ch. 13) seems to be a late attempt to make Samson respectable; none of his exploits show him as a religious enthusiast." Thus, the realization of the contradictions in the life of the Biblical Samson lead us to question Milton's choice of Samson as the typical believer whom he defends in the divorce tracts.

Before we begin to agree that Samson was a bad choice, there is more that we must understand. It seems that Milton, in choosing Samson, was following certain precedents. Milton's Samson is indeed a saint. According to Michael Krouse,

> During the first seven centuries of the Christian era a mass of hermeneutic literature from up around the four chapters of the Book of Judges, which chronicled the career of this religio-political hero of Judaism . . . there was the literal interpretation of the Samson story, decending from the Antiochan school of historio-grammatical exegesis, which sometimes took the form of mere retelling without explicit interpretation which included rhetorical use of Samson in arguments in favor of chastity, and which resulted in the conception of Samson as saint, necessitating an explanation of his fall and redemption.[3]

Those who thought of Samson as a saint remembered the reference to him in Hebrews 11

> where he is numbered among the patriarchs of the Old Testament, men who were all saints, in the Pauline sense, that is, electi, true believers, men distinguished by their good faith.[4]

Krouse recognizes Athanasius (d. 373) as "the earliest explicit indication that Christian thinkers would take up Samson as a saint."[5] Athanasius, in his Ad Episcopos Aegyptii et Libyae Epistola, "spoke of David, Samuel, and Samson together as ἅγιοι, saints or holy men, who had always been revered because they suffered death for their devotion to God."[6] Samson was a name worthy to be mentioned. Both Ambrose and Chrysostom had definite ideas about Samson:

> In the fourth century, Ambrose wrote a lengthy homily in the form of an epistle to his friend Virgilius, Bishop of Trent, in which Samson's entire career is reviewed to demonstrate the evils of marriage between Christian and infidel. Ambrose made it plain that even his being a Nazarite consecrated to God, attended by the Holy Spirit, and endowed with superhuman strength and zeal did not save Samson from the perils and sorrows lying in wait for him who takes an alien woman in marriage.[7]

Chrysostom, in one of his homilies, is said to have "defended the inclusion of Samson among the holy fathers of the Old Testament, arguing that the less savory events of his life do not matter because he believed and was resplendent in faith."[8] Hence, we have some insight about the appropriateness of Milton's choice of Samson as his example of the typical saint whose marriage to an infidel breaks his relationship with God and causes him to suffer a spiritual retrogression which is only cured by divorce.

The purpose of relating these specifics about Milton's Samson is to show that Milton was primarily interested in a story with a character capable of typifying a believer, dedicated to God first, a follower of charity, whose bad choice in marriage proved that the "rule of charity" must be the sovereign rule in deciding upon divorce. With the necessary accomodations, Samson plays that role well. One should not become involved in trying to solve the seeming "paradox" in the life of the Biblical Samson. Although references are made to Samson's past, only his past marriage to Dalila, included by Milton, is important. In Milton's creation of Samson, Samson, not God, moves himself to marry the "unfit" Dalila. It is with Dalila "that Samson operated outside providence."[9] <u>Samson Agonistes</u> must be interpreted only by the material that Milton included from his source and added from the resources of his own mind. Through Samson's past marriage to Dalila and the subsequent divorce, Milton effectively defends his argument in favor of divorce.

When Samson was married to Dalila, he had been faced with two things to consider, the love of God and the love of Dalila--the thing to be loved and the thing to be used. In the midst of making a decision, Samson, it seems, had forgotten the important dictum:

> If we who enjoy and use things, being placed in the midst of things of both kinds which should be used, our course shall be impeded and sometimes deflected, so that we are retarded in obtaining those things which are to be enjoyed, or even prevented altogether, shackled by an inferior love.[10]

Milton does not permit us, as he does in Paradise Lost, to view Samson and Dalila from the beginning of their marriage to the end. We meet the divorced Samson. Through Samson and other characters, we learn the details of Samson and Dalila's marriage. What we witness in Milton's account, the pain and mental anguish of a man who has been led astray by an unbelieving wife, is much more important. In the image of Samson, Milton actually presents a man who has been led astray by an "unfit" wife, but also one who regains his spiritual relationship with God through divorce, thus illustrating the good end of divorce when it restores a man to spiritual communion. Very few persons who had read Milton's divorce tracts had understood just how the "rule of charity" works to unbind the tormented husband from an unspiritual situation, or that to prohibit divorce was to honor matrimony above religion and charity. A major concern of Milton's in Samson Agonistes is the good end of divorce. Through self-analysis, after the divorce, Samson is victorious in his quest of eternal salvation. As the "rule of charity" has justified Samson's divorce of Dalila, charity above all things comes to be a central theme in the contest between the God of Israel and Dagon, the god of the Philistines. By defeating Dagon, Samson proves that his return to God and his love for Him is again complete.

The Samson who sits before the prison in Gaza acknowledges

his sin of disloyalty to God, the substitution of a love of matrimony for the love of God. This self-analysis begins with a recapitulation of his preordained relationship with God.

> O wherefore was my birth from Heaven foretold
> Twice by an Angel, who at last in sight
> Of both my Parents all in flames ascended
> From off the Altar, where an offering burn'd,
> As in a fiery column charioting
> Has God like presence, and from some great act
> Or benefit reveal'd to Abraham's race?
> Why was my breeding order'd and prescrib'd
> As of a person separate to God,
> Designed for great exploits, if I must die
> Betray'd, captiv'd, and both my Eyes put out,
> Made of my Enemies the scorn and gaze;
> To grind in Brazen fetters under task
> With this Heav'n gifted strength?
> 25-36

But even while Samson asks these questions, one gets the impression that Samson has the answers. He knows that he is to blame for what has happened:

> Whom have I to complain of but myself?
> Who this high gift of strength committed to one,
> In what part lodg'd, how easily bereft me,
> Under the seal of silence could not keep,
> But weakly to a woman must reveal it,
> O'er come with importunity and tears.
> O impotence of mind, in body strong!
> 46-52

Samson had failed to keep Dalila in the proper perspective as "a thing to be used" in the attainment of his own spiritual victory. Even those who choose to believe that God prompted Samson to marry Dalila would have to acknowledge Dalila as "a thing to be used." Since Dalila was a worshiper of Dagon, it was more important for Samson to see her as a <u>possible</u> "thing to be used," because, to begin with, Dalila was "unfit" as a spiritual companion. Milton did not believe too much in the Pauline ideology of marrying one who does not believe, with the hope of converting the person. There is danger in doing this. In the divorce tracts, Milton clarifies that a "fit" mate is one capable of providing "apt and cheerful conversation" which must first be related to charity. Dalila did not have those qualities that make a wife fit to be "used." In the divorce tracts, Milton argued that the harmonious marriage was one in which both individuals love God together. The spiritual relationship between man and wife must be similar to that between fellow-men:

> When you enjoy a man in God, it is God rather than the man whom you enjoy, for you take joy in Him who will make you blessed, and you will rejoice that you have reached Him in whom you place your hope that you may come.[11]

To apply St. Augustine's doctrine, Milton would say that the thing which a man ought to enjoy in his wife is God, as it is God who makes him blessed, not his wife. The wife is a means by which he reaches God: she is able to share the spiritual experience with her husband. The lvoe of Christ and the mind of Christ that dwells in the wife makes her a thing fit to be used in her husband's attainment of spiritual salvation.

Milton proves that Dalila was unfit for Samson and that an unbelieving wife will eventually "disinable [her husband] in the whole service of God through the disturbance of her unhelpful and unfit society."[12] Samson's marriage to such an individual as Dalila proved that "to enjoyn the indissoluble keeping of a marriage found unfit against the good of man both soul and body, as has been evident, is to make an Idol of mariage, to advance it above the worship of God and the good of man."[13]

After bemoaning his past sinful action, Samson curses his blindness, one of the results of his sin. However, there is more to the mentioning of his blindness. In the Scripture, the differences between light and darkness are the differences between wisdom and ignorance. Let us not forget Samson's earlier reference to his "impotence of mind." Samson's blindness symbolizes his mental blindness, or spiritual blindness, for wisdom is to know God and to love Him above all things. Thus, the physical blindness that Samson talks about, while pointing to his spiritual blindness, verifies that Samson's relationship with God has been broken. Samson describes light as "the prime work of God," a gift once granted to him by God, but now taken. He cries aloud

> O dark, dark, dark, amid the blaze of noon,
> Irrecoverably dark, total Eclipse
> Without all hope of day!
> O first created Beam, and thou great Word,
> "Let there be light, and light was over all";
> Why am I thus bereav'd thy prime decree? . . .
> Since light is so necessary to life,
> And almost life itself, if it be true,
> That light is in the Soul,
> She all in every part.
> 81-86; 90-93

At this point, Samson feels that the loss of sight is "worse than chains." Later he says "that which was the worst now least afflicts me,/Blindness, for had I sight, confus'd with shame,/How could I once look up . . .?" (195-7) We are not to think of this latter utterance as contradictory, because the closer Samson comes to regaining spiritual insight, the less painful it is to be physically blind. His willingness to accept his physical blindness shows his personal shame of having disobeyed his God. He thinks that he is probably "sung and proverb'd for a Fool/In every street." When a man fails the test of Godly love, he endangers his soul and loses his spiritual wisdom. The Chorus reminds Samson:

> thy Soul. . .
> Imprison'd now indeed,
> In real darkness of the body dwells,
> Shut up from outward light
> To incorporate with gloomy night;
> For inward light, alas,
> Puts forth no visual beam.
> 156; 158-63

St. Augustine would have interpreted that "inward light" as charity spread within by the Holy Spirit. In his <u>Homilies on the Gospel of St. John</u>, he writes that the "soul, if it be without the Holy Spirit, that is, without charity, will be reckoned dead."[14]   Samson, by succumbing to Dalila, had forsaken charity, the required love of God.

That divorce has been a good thing for Samson may be seen in his progression toward complete reunion with his God. There are several movements within this progression, each initiated by those who come to visit Samson: the Chorus, which is composed of his Israelite friends; Manoa, his father; Dalila, his ex-wife; and Harapha, a Philistine giant. In each confrontation, one feels the depth of Samson's sorrow for his sin of disobedience, his betrayal of the immutable love of God.

Samson's first extended reference to his past marital experiences is made while he talks with the Chorus:

> The first I saw at Timna, and she pleas'd
> Me, not my Parents, that I sought to wed,
> The daughter of an Infidel: they knew not
> That what I motion'd was of God; I knew
> From intimate impulse, and therefore urg'd
> The Marriage on; that by occasion hence
> I might begin Israel's Deliverance,
> The work to which I was divinely call'd;
> She proving false, the next I took to wife
> (O that I never had! fond wish too late)
> Was in the Vale of Sorec, Dalila,
> That specious Monster, my accomplisht snare
> I thought it lawful from my former act,
> And the same end; still watching to oppress
> Israel's oppressors: of what now I suffer
> She was not the prime cause, but I myself
> Who vanquisht with a peal of words (O weakness!)
> Gave up my fort of silence to a Woman.
>   219-36

The point of having Samson speak of his marriage to the woman of Timna, followed by reference to Dalila, is that Samson's error in marrying Dalila cannot be attributed to divine inspiration. It "seemed" to Samson the right thing to do, for the same purposes as before. In the Biblical version of the Samson story, there are no indications that God inspired Samson to go in to the harlot or to take Dalila as his mistress. In each case, the woman was chosen by Samson; therefore, it becomes fitting for

Milton to present Samson as having been married to Dalila, for
thematic purposes. Milton is cognizant of the wrong assumption that many will make when reference is made to the woman
of Timna along with Dalila. Samson accepts the fact that his
marriage to Dalila was his mistake and that the chances of his
betrayal were evident from the moment he set eyes on her. It is
important for Samson, in his progression, to be able to detect
the point at which he went wrong.

    The second movement in the spiritual progression of Samson
is brought about through his confrontation with his father, Manoa.
Samson has already determined the cause of his pain and suffering. Manoa leads him to a profound realization of his disloyalty to God, an indication, at the time, of his decreased love for
God. As for Samson's bad marriage, Manoa did not agree to it
from the beginning, but he is willing to let bygones be bygones:

> I cannot praise thy marriage choice, Son,
> Rather approv'd them not; but thou didst plead
> Divine impulsion prompting thou might'st
> Lead some occasion to infest our Foes.
>   420-23

Manoa had accepted Samson's explanation of the marriage. Manoa
realizes that the mistake has been made and cannot be changed.
Samson must, instead of apologizing, deal with the tragic result
of his sin--a broken relationship with God. The one true God must
be declared as such by Samson, since his sin has brought about the
occasion of the feast in honor of Dagon, the victorious god. Manoa
sees the horror of it all:

>   A worse thing yet remains.
> This day the Philistines a popular Feast
> Here celebrate in Gaza; and proclaim
> Great Pomp, and Sacrifice, and Praises loud
> To Dagon, as their God who hath deliver'd
> Thee, Samson, bound and blind into their hands,
> Them out of thine, who slew'st them many a slain
> So Dagon shall be magnified, and God
> Besides whom is no God, compar'd with Idols,

> Disglorified, blasphem'd, and had in scorn
> By the Idolatrous rout amidst their wine
> Which to have come to pass by means of thee,
> Samson, of all thy sufferings think the heaviest,
> Of all reproach the most with shame that ever
> Could have befall'n thee and thy Father's house.
>   434-48

According to the commandment (Exodus 20:3), man is commanded by God to have no other gods before Him, and in later explanation (Deuteronomy 6:5), we learn that man must "love the Lord with all [his] heart, and with all [his] soul, and with all [his] might." This is what the "rule of charity" is all about and this is the rule that Samson broke when he disobeyed God in favor of Dalila. Just as in Samson's marriage the contest had been between God and Dalila, it is now the contest between God and Dagon. In the first contest, Samson failed to choose God above Dalila; but, in this ongoing contest between God and Dagon, Samson must show God to be victorious over Dagon. In the past, Samson

>   brought
> Dishonor, obloquy, and op't the mouthes
> Of Idolists, and Atheists . . . brought scandal
> To Israel, diffidence to God, and doubt
> To feeble hearts, propense enough before
> To waver, or fall off and join with Idols.
>   451-6

To Manoa, Samson conveys his "chief affliction, shame, sorrow,/ The anguish of [his] Soul." All has been a "blot/To Honor and Religion." Samson must "vindicate the glory of [God's] name/ Against all competition." It is Manoa who leads Samson to talk about the heinousness of his crime, disloyalty to God, the choice of matrimony over God, the result of Samson's inability to distinguish between two things, the love of God and the love of Dalila--the thing to be loved and the thing to be used. Samson remembers:

> into the snare I fell
> Of fair fallacious looks, venereal trains
> Soft'n'd with pleasure and voluptous life;
> At length to lay my head and hallow'd pledge
> Of all my strength in the lascivious lap
> Of a deceitful concubine who shore me
> Like a tame Wether, all my precious fleece,
> Then turn'd me out ridiculous, despoil'd,
> Shav'n, and disarm'd among my enemies.
> 531-40

Merritt Y. Hughes defines "venereal trains" as "tricks to arouse physical passion."[15]

    Milton believed that it would be difficult for a believer and an infidel to dwell in peace together, especially if the infidel shows no hope of conversion. Husbands who had to live with such circumstances lived in danger of spiritual chaos. In this state, a man is likely to turn from God; and, once he turns from God, his mind is tormented by the pain of his spiritual loss. This is the case of Samson.

> Thoughts my Tormentors arm'd with deadly stings
> Mingle my apprehensive tenderest parts,
> Exasperate, exulcerate, and raise
> Dire inflammation which no cooling herb
> Or med'cinal liquor can assuage,
> Nor breath of Vernal Air from snowy Alp.
> Sleep hath forsook and giv'n me o'er
> To death's benumbing Opium as my only cure.
> Thence faintings, swoonings of despair,
> And sense of Heav'n's desertion.
> 623-32

Now that Samson has correctly interpreted the value of what he once had, he is on his way to a complete spiritual renewal through his determination to declare his God almighty indeed.

    The third movement in Samson's progression toward spiritual reunion is seen in his forcefulness during his encounter with Dalila, his ex-wife. Samson understands Dalila for what she *is*, no different than she was before the divorce, still unfit as an aid to his spiritual renewal. It is in this third movement that Milton takes the opportunity to argue his case in favor of divorce.

His distrust of the unbelieving wife becomes more and more evident. In <u>Tetrachordon</u>, while defending his position against continued marriage with an infidel, Milton expounded upon St. Paul's lesson in I Cor. 7:12 (RSV), "To the rest I say, not the Lord, that if any brother has a wife who is an unbeliever, and she consents to live with him, he should not divorce her." Although Milton makes certain concessions to this Pauline ideology, he seems somewhat wary of it, as we sense from the following words:

> if we turne not hope into bondage, the charitable and free hope of gaining another, into the force't and servile temptation of losing our selves . . . not the law only, but the Gospel from the law, and from it selfe requires even in the same chapter, where divorce between them of one religion is so narrowly forbidd, rather than our christian love should come in danger of backsliding, to forsake all relations how neer so ever, the wife expresly, with promise of a high reward, Mat. 19. And he who hates not father and mother, wife or children hindering his Christian cours, much more, if they despise or assault it, cannot be a Disciple, Luke 14. How can the Apostle then command us, to love and continue in that matrimony, which our Saviour bids us hate, and forsake?[16]

Milton's distrust of an infidel wife is manifested in Samson's encounter with Dalila. Samson stands firmly grounded in his determination to become reunited in love with the Father and to make his divorce from Dalila permanent. Samson sees the insincerity of Dalila and her unfitness as a "thing to be used." It is likely that Samson's firmness of determination has been reenforced by his recent encounter with his father, who showed great sorrow for Samson's betrayal of the God of Israel, the one true God. To be trapped by the same snare would be a guarantee of Samson's defeat.

Milton's Dalila is capable of misleading the reader into thinking that her sorrow is sincere, but not of misleading Samson. Her first speech to Samson is one of seeming penance. She acknowledges her sin and pretends that her "penance hath not slacken'd."

Her excuse for visiting Samson is a sympathetic one:

> conjugal affection,
> Prevailing over fear and timorous doubt
> Hath led me on desirous to behold
> Once more thy face, and know of thy estate.
> If aught in my ability may serve
> To light'n what thou suffer'st, and appease
> Thy mind with what amends is in my power,
> Though late, yet in some part to recompense
> My rash but most unfortunate misdeed.
> 740-48

In Samson's firm response, one can somehow feel the presence of Milton:

> Out, out Hyaena; these are thy wonted arts.
> And arts of every woman false like thee,
> To break all faith, all vows, deceive, betray,
> Then as repentant to submit, beseech,
> And reconcilement move with feign'd remorse,
> Confess, and promise wonders in her change,
> Not truly penitent, but chief to try
> Her husband, how far urg'd his patience bears,
> His virtue or weakness which way to assail:
> Then with more cautious and instructed skill
> Again transgresses, and again submits;
> That wisest and best men full oft beguil'd,
> With goodness principl'd not to reject
> The penitent, but ever to forgive,
> Are drawn to wear out miserable days,
> Entangl'd with a pois'nous bosom snake.
> 748-63

Some scholars have taken this passage as proof of Milton's misogny, but one must realize that such a reading is not well justified. After all, Milton's marital experiences were not, in any way, as painful as those of Samson. These words are appropriate for what Samson has experienced and they are uttered in anger and perturbation. Samson is determined that he will not be deceived again: he is sure that Dalila is "unfit" to share the love that he has for the one true God.

Dalila's method of attempted deception is to repeat the same "seeming" penitent line, acknowledging her sinful deed, but declaring that she deserves pardon. She also listens carefully to

Samson's speeches, so that she might know how to choose her strategy. She is not bothered by being placed in a class with deceitful women. She admits that certain traits such as curiosity and inquisitiveness are characteristic of "all our sex." Dalila's insincerity however soon comes to surface when she suggests to Samson, "Let weakness then with weakness come to parle." This indicates that she really excuses her betrayal of Samson. She still has no basic understanding of what her responsibilities as a wife were to Samson: to help nurture the love of God in him and provide the peaceful atmosphere in which he might commune with God. In her plea for pardon, Dalila's excuse of wanting Samson all to herself automatically excludes any respect for Samson's God. In Dalila's complete revelation of insincerity, one understands that Dalila is a true worshiper of Dagon:

> It was not gold, as to my charge thou lay'st
> That wrought with me: thou knowst the Magistrates
> And princes of my Country came in person,
> Solicited, commanded, threat'n'd, urg'd,
> Adjur'd by all the bonds of Civil Duty
> And of Religion, press'd how just it was,
> How honorable, how glorious to entrap
> A common enemy, who had destroy'd
> Such numbers of our Nation: and the Priest
> Was not behind, but ever at my ear,
> Preaching how meritorious with the gods
> It would be to ensnare an irreligious
> Dishonorer of Dagon: what had I
> To oppose against such powerful arguments?
> 849-62

What a loyal wife would have had to oppose "such powerful arguments" should have been her loyalty to her husband. Although Dalila had been the daughter of an infidel and an infidel herself, her intentions--when she married Samson--should have been to unite with her husband in the love of his God. Milton's skepticism of the Pauline ideology, regarding the retention of an unbelieving wife who desires to remain with her husband, seems to be well founded in the Samson-Dalila episodes. The soul is too precious to be placed in such spiritual danger. Samson reminds Dalila:

>   had the love, still odiously pretended,
> Been, as it ought, sincere, it would have taught thee
> Far other reasonings, brought forth other deeds . . . .
> Being once a wife, for me thou wast to leave
> Parents and country . . .
> But zeal moved thee;
> To please thy gods thou didst it; gods unable
> To acquit themselves and prosecute their foes
> But by ungodly deeds, the contradiction
> Of their owne deity, Gods cannot be:
> Less therefore to be pleas'd, obey'd, or fear'd.
>   873-75; 885-6; 895-900

Each confrontation makes Samson realize more and more his loss in being deceived by Dalila, thereby strengthening his determination to be reunited with the Father. Samson's total energy is directed toward this spiritual end. As for Samson, the divorce is permanent:

>   No, no, of my condition take no care;
> It fits not; thou and I long since are twain'
> Nor think me so unwary or accurst
> To bring my feet again into the snare
> Where once I have been caught.
>   927-31

Dalila's deception is discovered and defeated. She must admit that she chose "above the faith of wedlock bonds" and that she rejoices in being honored as "the famousest/Of Women" in her country.

Much has been accomplished in Samson's confrontation with Dalila. Throughout the confrontation, Milton has expounded upon the "rule of charity" in matrimony, just as he did in the divorce tracts. The husband must love God above his wife. If it should come to a choice between the two, God must be chosen. A wife must be the "fit" individual capable of sharing with her husband the love of God. In the case of Samson and Dalila, while Samson talks of the God of Israel, Dalila feels compelled to talk of Dagon. In Samson's fall, we are able to see just what happened to the man who remained with an "unfit" wife. It is only after the divorce that Samson, after self-analysis, begins his journey back to the God of Israel. In the divorce tracts, Milton proposed that divorce steps be taken the moment that the signs of trouble appear, in order that the soul be protected. In Samson's refusal of Dalila, Milton is able to reemphasize the "rule of charity" as the husband's sole protector.

The fourth movement in the progression of Samson toward spiritual reunion involves his confrontation with the Philistine giant, Harapha, a worshiper of Dagon. It has been conjectured that this confrontation symbolizes Milton's literary and philosophical battle with Salmasius, a contemporary who advocated the crown in his <u>Defensio regia pro Carlo I ad regem Carolum II</u> in retaliation against Milton's advocation of regicide. According to William R. Parker,

> Such was the philosophy of regicide which Milton offered in <u>The Tenure of Kings</u>. He did not debate the guilt of Charles I; indeed, he carefully avoided any reference to the late King by name. The trial had been the business of others. His own concern was to justify the judging.[17]

It seems to me, however, that this scene between Samson and Harapha is rather a continued commentary on the "rule of charity."

From the beginning, Samson has been cognizant of the fact that he must love God foremost. It just happened that, in the language of St. Augustine, he faltered on his course. It is after the fall and divorce that he is more aware of the fact that he really must love God above all things and creatures. To Milton, there is but one supreme being and that is God. Thus, everything that happens following the visit of Manoa shows Samson moving toward the full reaffirmation of his first love of God. Harapha represents Dagon, and Samson represents God; therefore, the combat that Samson challenges Harapha with is evidence of his intense desire to do the ultimate to reaffirm his love for God. To Harapha, Samson says

> I know no spells, use no forbidden Arts;
> My trust is in the living God who gave me
> At my Nativity this strength, diffus'd
> No less through all my sinews, joints and bones,
> Than thine, while I preserv'd these locks unshorn,

> The pledge of my unviolated vow.
> For proof hereof, if Dagon be thy god,
> Go to his Temple, invocate his aid
> With solmnest devotion, spread before him
> How highly it concerns his glory now
> To frustrate and dissolve these magic spells,
> Which I to be the power of Israel's God
> Avow, and challenge Dagon to the test,
> Offering to combat thee his Champion bold,
> With the utmost of his Godhead seconded:
> Then thou shalt see, or rather to thy sorrow
> Soon feel, whose God is strongest, thine or mine.
>   1139-55

These lines indicate the culmination of Samson's repentence and spiritual revival. These words spoken by Samson refer us back to those words spoken by Manoa earlier:

>   for God,
> Nothing more certain, will not long defer
> To vindicate the glory of his name
> Against all competition, nor will long
> Endure it, doubtful whether God be Lord
> Or Dagon.
>   473-78

Harapha is a test of the degree of Samson's spiritual recovery. Harapha says to Samson:

> Presume not on thy God, what'er he be,
> Thee he regards not, owns not, hath cut off
> Quite from his people, and delivered up
> Into thy Enemies hand.
>   1156-59

Samson sounds very strong in his reply to Harapha. No longer does he ask the question, "To what end can I be useful"? He knows what he must do, for, although he remains physically blind, he is no longer spiritually blind:

> All these indignities, for such they are
> From thine, these evils I deserve and more,
> Acknowledge them from God inflicted on me
> Justly, yet despair not of his pardon
> Whose ear is ever open; and his eye
> Gracious to re-admit the suppliant;

> In confidence whereof I once again
> Defy thee to the trial of mortal fight,
> By combat to decide whose god is God,
> Thine or whom I with Israel's Sons adore.
> 1167-78

Samson will pass the test.

Keeping in mind the meaning of this confrontation with Harapha, let us now turn our attention to Samson's invitation to perform at the feast given in honor of Dagon. His first response to the invitation is negative:

> Can they think me broken, so debas'd
> With corporal servitude, that my mind ever
> Will condescend to such absurd commands?
> Although thir drudge, to be thir fool or jester,
> And in my midst of sorrow and heart grief
> To show them feats, and play before thir god,
> The worst of all indignities, yet on me
> Join'd with extreme contempt. I will not come.
> 1335-42

As a result of having lost his "Consecrated gift" because he submitted to an inferior love, Samson cherishes the "favor renew'd." To bow to Dagon would be to have another god before the one true God. He would be forsaking charity and falling into the same snare that caught him before. Samson's first thought is that to perform before Dagon would be a public denial of God. He has an afterthought, however, and "Some rousing motions" of Divine origin lead Samson to revoke his earlier answer. The invitation is his chance to publicly win victory for his God. He decides to go to the feast of Dagon. His words are:

> I with this Messenger will go along,
> Nothing to do, be sure, that may dishonor
> Our Law, or stain my vow of Nazarite.
> 1383-85

And

> Happ'n what may, of me expect to hear
> Nothing dishonorable, impure, unworthy
> Our God, our Law, my Nation, or myself.
> 1423-25

Samson is now a Nazarite in the true sense of the word. Proper order has returned: he will do nothing to dishonor God, the Law, the Nation, or himself.

Samson's urge to go before the Philistines at Gaza was evidence of Samson's complete love of God and of his belief that God could use him "in some great service." Dagon falls, but the God of Israel stands victorious. Samson falls physically, but he rises spiritually.

One of Milton's arguments in the divorce tracts had been that the permission of men of the Old Testament to divorce their wives was not abrogated by the words of Christ in the New Testament. It then becomes significant that Samson is an Old Testament character. Through Samson's divorce, Milton makes a profound statement to his contemporaries. What was good for believers of the Old Testament must be good for believers of the New Testament. Divorce, sanctioned by the "rule of charity," remains the only hope of the believer who is unfortunately married to an infidel. Through the speeches of Samson and of others, during the period of Samson's progression toward renewed faith and reunion with God, Milton explicitly explains the justifiable reasons for Samson's divorce of Dalila. Through retrospection, Samson and others assure us that Dalila was not the wife capable of being used by her husband in his attainment of eternal salvation. It is because we know this that we can appreciate the concentration upon Samson's progression toward spiritual renewal. The entire body of <u>Samson Agonistes</u> deals with the lesson of charity in an extreme sort of way. Divorce leads Samson to a greater love of God.

Samson benefits from his mistakes. He realizes that his marriage to Dalila was the beginning of his fall, as he saw Dalila in the wrong perspective, not as a "thing to be used" but rather as a "thing to be loved." Charity was not the rule of their house. Samson's regeneration depended upon a reversed order, where the love of God supersedes all relationships. The moment Samson left Dalila behind is the moment when the process of regeneration began, the moment when he began to tread his way back to God.[18] Actually, Samson "attains to union with God by way of the apparently negative path of divorcing his wife."[19] Of course, the path is only negative for those who do not understand the "rule of charity" as it operates in the marriage union. The path is a positive one for Milton, who had said in his divorce tracts that any law which forbids a man to divorce an "unfit" wife is against nature and an unnatural law. Milton would agree that if divorce "dissolved a marriage that has been attempted <u>contra</u> <u>naturam</u>," it "actually restores right order by recognizing that an unremediable spiritual disjunction exists."[20]

Milton's decision that divorce must be granted on grounds of spiritual incompatibility was a sound orthodox decision, and to defend this decision with the "rule of charity" has no firmer basis than St. Augustine's original exegesis of <u>caritas</u> in the works that I have already mentioned. When I use the word <u>orthodox</u>, I am not using it in the sense of some thought that had been sanctioned by the Christian church of Milton's time. Rather, I am using the word to mean that which makes good sense. As for Milton, if a marriage is not spiritual in nature, it cannot serve any good end. The husband must be for God and the wife must be for God in her husband. Through the Samson-Dalila exemplum, Milton has given many reasons for divorce on due cause and for its justification in the "rule of charity."

VI

Conclusion

In the preceding chapters, the central thesis has been that John Milton's "rule of charity" teaches a doctrine of use which must be operative in the marriage between believers, or otherwise divorce of the party who makes it inoperative is justifiable. In the marriage between believers, each individual must love God above all things and see the other as "a thing to be used"--a means of attaining spiritual union with God. The same "rule of charity" which has the power to make a marriage happy also has the power to dissolve the marriage in which one individual fails to be "a thing to be used," and instead remains "a thing unfit to be used." In developing this thesis, I have set out to prove several points: that Milton's concept of charity bears much resemblance to St. Augustine's exegesis of <u>caritas</u> in several of his works, especially <u>De Doctrina Christiana</u>; that Milton's "rule of charity" is scripturally sound and therefore far from unorthodox--as the Christian church of Milton's time characterized it; and that <u>Paradise Lost</u> and <u>Samson Agonistes</u> are definite exempla of Milton's understanding of how charity works to keep a marriage happy and of how charity must be the sovereign determinant of whether of not divorce is scripturally justified.

It is not surprising that Milton's understanding of charity as it operates in marriage and in divorce should bear general resemblance with St. Augustine's explanation of charity. My aim is not to suggest St. Augustine as a source for so fundamental a Christian concept as charity, but rather as a source of the exegesis of charity. In theological terms, there is obviously no source of charity outside of God. There were many churchmen besides St. Augustine, for example Chrysostom, Jerome, Ambrose, and Anthony, who often commented on the commandment of love; but, St. Augustine stands out as a demonstrable exegete, whose voice as the "Protestant Father" gives his commentary a special claim to attention.

As M. Huftier states, "S. Augustine peut sans contredit être appelé le docteur de la charité."[1] St. Augustine spoke at length about "l'origine divine de la grace et de la charité" and "l'opposition entre charité et cupiditié." He felt that "la charité est une dette dont il faut sans cesse s'acquitter sans pourvoir jamais la payer entierement."[2] During the Middle Ages and on into the Renaissance, St. Augustine was the most accepted authority on Christian doctrine. As Henri Marrou states:

> This presence of St. Augustine in the midst of the culture of the last few generations, and of our own, is so easily perceived that there is no need to produce proofs of it. He remains one of the few Christian thinkers of whose existence non-Christians are aware, and to whom they allow a place, at least, in the evolution of the human mind. Protestantism has never ceased to be interested in him, however far from his doctrinal and ecclesiastical positions it has proved itself to be, especially when liberalism was dominant, and it even disputes his patronage in some respects with Catholicism.[3]

That there is such resemblance between St. Augustine's and Milton's concept of charity is not without reason, for--as I stated earlier--a theological scholar such as Milton could not escape knowledge of St. Augustine and his major works.

The seeming oddity of Milton's "rule of charity" as it is applied to marriage and to divorce vanishes when it is placed along side St. Augustine's exegesis. Not only does one begin to see the beauty of that marriage in which both husband and wife love God above all things, but one also begins to see the obvious immorality, irrationality, and unnaturalness of forcing a man to live in a situation which will eventually lead to a broken relationship with God. As fellow-men must "use" each other as means of reaching God, so must husband and wife "use" each other in reaching a perfect union with God. In the case that Milton has presented, a woman's mental capacity must be the first consideration of a man who seeks a marriage partner. In a more important way, Milton sees the woman as a "thing to be used" by man in his spiritual endeavors. The woman with a good mind is a woman who is capable of furthering her husband's spiritual life and who finds her salvation through her husband. In Milton's language, such a woman is indeed a "fit" helpmeet.

This study aims to show that it was not Milton's application of the "rule of charity" to marriage and divorce that was absurd, but rather the bondage of the Canon Law. How could the Canon Law sanction, as it must have, the Christian command of charity--to love God with the <u>whole</u> heart, <u>whole</u> soul, and <u>whole</u> mind, above all things--and, at the same time, refuse to allow divorce in a marriage where one party hinders the other from fulfilling the command of charity? This, for Milton, was the greatest contradiction.

It is from Milton's divorce tracts that one learns what the ingredients of a happy marriage are. I have pointed out that, in such a marriage, the couple worships God above all things. The husband is the spiritual leader and the wife is his helper. The wife may either further or hinder her husband's spiritual progress. If she becomes a hindrance, she is classified as an infidel and worthy to be divorced by her husband, such divorce being justified by the Christian command of charity. Milton makes it clear that no man should be penalized for not being sure of his choice in marriage, for--as he says--the wisest of men have erred in choosing.

I have noted that Milton had problems in presenting his proposal for divorce, which he hoped to defend scripturally with the Christian commandment of love, primarily because of the seeming contradiction between the Old Testament and the New Testament. Those individuals who did not accept Milton's proposal justified their opposition by referring to Christ's words to the Pharisees' inquiry regarding divorce. According to Milton, Christ curbed one extremity with another extremity: the Pharisees had been known to divorce their wives for any trivial reason; therefore, their divorce privileges were revoked. Milton saw no real problem between the two testaments: Christ could not have abrogated the Mosaic Law, for Christ came to fulfill the Law. The Mosaic Law had been a guide to moral living and Christ did not introduce so much any new morality as rather "Christian liberty." Milton emphasized throughout the divorce tracts, as he defended his position, that God cannot be contradictory and neither can the Scripture. Many scriptural problems are best solved by using one scripture to explain another. Charity was the new commandment, the fulfillment of the whole Law, and every scripture had to coincide with this command.

After looking at Milton's <u>Doctrine and Discipline of Divorce</u>, <u>Tetrachordon</u>, and passages from <u>De Doctrina Christiana</u>, one must conclude that Milton's view of marriage was a spiritual one, and that it was only because of this that he could propose divorce on grounds of spiritual incompatibility. From all that has been presented, it is difficult for me to understand how Milton could ever be accused of insincerity and of using anything, even the Bible, to justify his own personal intentions. The only subjectivism that one readily sees in the divorce tracts is the male point of view. Milton was indeed sincere and his sincerity has been shown to have extended beyond the divorce tracts into his poetry.

In the latter part of this study, I have concentrated on two of Milton's poetic works as exempla of Milton's view on marriage and divorce. While <u>Paradise Lost</u>, Milton's masterpiece, is an exemplum of the good marriage and of the bad marriage, <u>Samson Agonistes</u>, a dramatic piece, has been shown as an exemplum of the positive good of divorce when it leads to a spiritual end.

The marriage of Adam and Eve began in the right way: it was ordained and sanctioned by God. Both persons realized their first duty to God. Adam and Eve are shown, in the prelapsarian state, to be spiritually and physically content persons. Their state of being is a happy one, because they are obedient to God and are able to appreciate His creation surrounding them. Adam and Eve work side by side and all goes well primarily because Eve follows Adam, always trusting him as her leader. Not only have we seen a unity of mind in Adam and Eve but also a unified order in surrounding Nature. Milton used the first eight books of <u>Paradise Lost</u> to show the ingredients of a happy marriage: Adam never forgets the difference between the "thing to be loved" and the "thing to be used." Both husband and wife are headed in the direction of Heaven.

It is in Book IX, as I have sought to show, that Milton presents us with the ingredients of a bad marriage. As obedience has been the sign of love for God, disobedience becomes the sign of a lack of love for God above all things. Eve developed a will of her own and became the infidel that Milton talked so much about in the divorce tracts. I have described Eve's departure from Adam as symbolic of her departure from God. In Adam's subsequent compliance with Eve, Milton has proved that divorce is necessary for the spiritual protection of the believing party of a marriage. Adam's inability to divorce himself from Eve brings him nothing but pain and the horror of sin, with the constant realization of his once happy state. In the last two books of <u>Paradise Lost</u>, Milton's intentions seem to have been to re-establish in the minds of his readers that the "rule of charity" is of prime importance as the sovereign rule in marriage, as it is in every other phase of life.

The second poetic exemplum chosen for discussion was <u>Samson Agonistes</u>, which deals primarily with the subject of divorce. Marriage is a subject in retrospect. My aim was to show Samson to be the typical saint whom Milton defended in the divorce tracts--a saint led astray by an "unfit" wife. In Samson we are able to get an extended look at the pain and suffering of a man who realized his sin of disloyalty to God--a sign of his having loved something or someone above God. Milton made it clear through retrospection that, from the beginning, Dalila had been an "unfit" wife for Samson, that she had not been a "thing fit to be used" in Samson's spiritual endeavors. In other words, the fact that Dalila was an infidel and Samson was a believer in the God of Israel made it impossible for there to exist in their marriage a mental union. In <u>Samson Agonistes</u>, Milton's major concentration seems to have been the good end of divorce. As a result, the "rule of charity" was brought to the forefront in the contest between Dagon and the God of Israel. It seems clear that Samson fell because he substituted his love for God with his love for

Dalila, which was really a love for Dagon, as Dalila was a worshiper of Dagon. It is because Samson realized the horror of his sin that he understood that his complete reunion with God had to be accomplished through his physical defeat. He had to declare his God of Israel victorious over Dagon. In the final analysis, Samson's spiritual success followed his divorce from Dalila.

As I compare these two works, I think that both are great exempla of Milton's ideas, but that <u>Samson</u> <u>Agonistes</u>, in its unusual way, is a more forceful commentary on divorce as a positive moral action, justified by Scripture. With <u>Paradise</u> <u>Lost</u>, it seems that one might easily forget the period of time during which Adam and Eve experience a bad marriage, simply because there is a spiritual beginning and a spiritual ending. Despite this fact, Eve shall forever stand as the prototypal symbol of the "unfit" wife who disobeyed her husband and God. Her sin and her penalty became the sin and the penalty of all women. Hence, those of us who castigate Milton for what seems to be a one-sided argument in favor of the husband must realize that Milton's perception of women is an historical perception--suported both by the Bible and his culture. <u>Paradise</u> <u>Lost</u>, then, serves more as an exemplum of the good marriage and the "fit wife," while <u>Samson</u> <u>Agonistes</u> seems to be Milton's authoritative word on divorce--the bad marriage and the "unfit" wife. In the final analysis, only divorce can cure the pain and anguish of the believing man who finds himself married to an unbelieving wife who shows no signs of changing

Our final estimate of John Milton and his "rule of charity" must take us in a new direction, away from the worn-out traditional explanations of Milton's reasons for writing the divorce tracts We must conclude that Milton's intentions were sincere, that he wished to show his countrymen that their negative thinking about divorce had been clouded by the dictates of custom and tradition, and that their opinions, however moral they may have sounded, were not founded upon any proper or right interpretation of the Scripture. The very chance that Milton took in publishing the divorce tracts was evidence of his belief that man's allegiance must be to God rather than to man, and that one's physical existence matters very little if spiritual contentedness is absent.

> Let not therefore the frailty of man goe
> on thus inventing needlesse troubles to
> itself to groan under the fals imagina-
> tion of a strictnes never impos'd from
> above, enjoyning that for duty which is
> an impossible and vain supererogating.[4]

Notes

Chapter I

¹John Milton, "The Christian Doctrine," *John Milton: Complete Poems and Major Prose*, ed. Merritt Y. Hughes (New York: The Odyssey Press, 1957), p. 901.

²James Holly Hanford, "The Chronology of Milton's Private Studies," *PMLA*, XXXVI (March, 1921), 284. For more detailed information on Milton's references in the divorce tracts, see Frank Patterson, *An Index to the Columbia Edition of The Works of John Milton* (New York: Columbia University Press, 1940), Vols. I-II; to check the exact works of a certain person that Milton read, consult the index under the individual's name in *Complete Prose Works of John Milton*, II, ed. Ernest Sirluck (New Haven: Yale University Press; London: Oxford University Press, MCMLIX).

³Ibid., p. 258.

⁴Ibid., p. 284.

⁵Theodore L. Huguelet, *Milton's Hermeneutics: A Study of Scriptural Interpretation in the Divorce Tracts*, Diss. University of North Carolina, 1959, p. 9.

⁶For Milton's exact words, see *The Doctrine and Discipline of Divorce*, Book II, Chapter I, and Chapter XIX.

⁷Huguelet, loc. cit.

⁸Ibid., p. 253.

⁹Ibid., p. 254.

¹⁰cf. *The Doctrine and Discipline of Divorce*, Book I. Preface, and Book II, Chapter XVII. In the former reference, Milton describes Grotious as "a man of these times, one of the best learned," but, in the latter reference, he describes Grotius as "a man of general learning" -- a description that I accept.

¹¹C. A. Patrides, *Milton and the Christian Tradition* (Oxford: Clarendon Press, 1966), p. 3.

[12] James Basil Potts, <u>Milton's Deviations from Standard Biblical Interpretation in The Discussion of Divorce</u>, Diss. University of Mississippi, 1968, p. 56.

[13] <u>Ibid</u>., p. 120.

[14] <u>Ibid</u>., p. 174.

[15] See <u>The Doctrine and Discipline of Divorce</u>. Book II, Chapter XX.

[16] George Halkett, <u>Milton and the Idea of Matrimony</u>, Diss. Northwestern University, 1964 (New Haven: Yale University Press, 1970), p. 98.

[17] <u>Ibid</u>., p. 116.

Chapter II

[1] Translated, charity is "the motion of the soul toward the enjoyment of God for His own sake, and the enjoyment of one's self and of one's neighbor for the sake of God." Sancti Aurelii Augustini (Hipponensis Episcopi), <u>De Doctrina Christiana</u> in <u>Opera Omnia</u>, IV(Parisiis: Apud Gaume Fratres, Bibliopolas, M DCCC XXVI), (III, X, 16), 88. Translation by D. W. Robertson, ed., <u>On Christian Doctrine</u> (Indianapolis . New York: The Bobbs-Merrill Company, Inc., 1958). Hereafter referred to as DDC.

[2] <u>Ibid</u>. Translated, cupidity is "the motion of the soul toward the enjoyment of one's self, one's neighbor, or any corporal thing for the sake of something other than God."

[3] <u>Ibid</u>., (I, IV, 4), 22.

[4] <u>Ibid</u>., (I, III, 3).

[5] <u>Ibid</u>.

[6] John Burnaby, *Amor Dei: A Study of the Religion of St. Augustine* (London: Hudder and Stoughton, 1938), p. 115.

[7] *DDC, op. cit.*, (I, XXXIII, 37), 35.

[8] *Ibid.*, (I, XXIII, 22), 30.

[9] *Ibid.*, (I, V, 5), 22.

[10] *Ibid.*, (I, XXII, 20), 27.

[11] *Ibid.*, (I, IV, 4), 22.

[12] *Ibid.*, (I, XXII, 21), 30.

[13] *Ibid.*

[14] *Ibid.*, (I, XXVII, 28), 31.

[15] Edmund Spenser, "An Hymne of Heavenly Love," *The Complete Poetical Works of Spenser*, ed. R. E. Neil Dodge (Massachusetts: The Riverside Press, 1936), p. 750.

[16] *Ibid.*, p. 753.

[17] *Ibid.*, p. 755.

[18] *Ibid.*

[19] Plato, "Symposium," *Great Books of the Western World* (Chicago: William Benton, Publisher, 1952), VII, 158.

[20] *DDC, op. cit.*, (I, XXXV, 39), 38.

[21] *Ibid.*, (I, XXVI, 27), 35.

[22] *Ibid.*, (I, XXVI, 40), 38.

[23] Sancti Aurelii Augustini (Hipponensis Episcopi), *Enchiridion De Fide, Spe et Charitate* in *Opera Omnia*, Vol. III, Pt. 1 (Parisiis: Apud Gaume Fratres, Bibliopolas, M DCC XXXVII),

(31, CXVII), 406. Translation by J. F. Shaw in <u>Basic</u> <u>Writings</u> <u>of</u> <u>Saint</u> <u>Augustine</u>, ed. Whitney J. Oates (New York: Random House Publishers, 1948), I.

[24]Ibid., (32, CXXI), 407. cf. I Cor. 13; <u>Paradise</u> <u>Lost</u>, XII, 575-85.

[25]Sancti Aurelii Augustini (Hipponensis Episcopi), <u>In</u> <u>Joannis</u> <u>Evangelium</u> in <u>Opera</u> <u>Omnia</u>, Vol. III, Pt. II (Parisiis: Apud Gaume Fratres, Bibliopolas, M DCCC XXXVII), (Tractus IX, 8), 1786. Translation in St. Augustine, <u>Homilies</u> <u>on</u> <u>the</u> <u>Gospel</u> <u>of</u> <u>St.</u> <u>John</u>. <u>Homilies</u> <u>on</u> <u>the</u> <u>First</u> <u>Epistle</u> <u>of</u> <u>John</u>. <u>Soliloquies</u>. Ed. Philip Schaff (New York: The Christian Literature Company, 1888).

[26]Ibid., (Tractus XXXII, 9), 2030.

[27]Ibid.

[28]Ibid., (Tractus LXV, I), 2246.

[29]Ibid., (Tractus LXV, 2), 2247.

[30]Etiènne Gilson, <u>Introduction</u> <u>a</u> <u>L'Etude</u> <u>De</u> <u>Saint</u> <u>Augustin</u> (Paris: Librairie Philosophique, J. Vrin, 1929), p. 171. Translation my own.

[31]Ibid., see fn. 1, p. 171.

[32]Ibid., p. 173.

[33]Ibid., p. 174.

[34]Ibid., p. 176.

Chapter III

[1]Cf. Martin A. Larson, <u>The</u> <u>Modernity</u> <u>of</u> <u>Milton</u> (Chicago, Illinois: The University of Chicago Press, 1927), pp. 245, 248-9;

David Masson, The Life of John Milton (New York: Peter Smith, 1946), III, 42; Denis Saurat, Milton, Man and Thinker (London: J. M. Dent and Sons Ltd., 1946), p. 50; Arthur Barker, Milton and the Puritan Dilemna: 1641-1660 (Toronto: The University of Toronto Press, 1942), pp. 63-64; William Haller, "Hail Wedded Love," ELH, XIII (June, 1946), 79-97, esp. p. 80; William Haller, Liberty and Reformation in the Puritan Revolution (New York: Columbia University Press, 1955), p. 79; E. M. W. Tillyard, Milton (London: Chatto and Winders, 1956), p. 140; David Daiches, Milton (London: Hutchinson University Library, 1957), p. 114; Chilton L. Powell, "The Date and Occasion of Milton's First Divorce Tract," English Domestic Relations: 1487-1653 (New York: Columbia University Press, 1917), p. 227.

[2] See Arthur Barker, "Christian Liberty in Milton's Divorce Pamphlets," MLR, XXXV (April, 1940), 153-61, esp. p. 157; Arthur Barker, Milton and the Puritan Dilemma: 1641-1660 (Toronto: The University of Toronto Press, 1942), p. 72.

[3] John S. Diekhoff, Milton on Himself (New York: Oxford University Press, 1939), p. 23.

[4] Henre Smith, "Preparative to Marriage," The Sermons of Maister Henre Smith (London: Printed by Felix Kingston, 1957), pp. 24-25.

[5] Ibid., p. 37.

[6] Ibid.

[7] Ibid., pp. 37-8.

[8] Robert Cleaver, A Godlie Forme of Householde Government: for the Ordering of Private Families According to the Direction of Gods Word (London: Printed by Felix Kingston, 1598), p. 89.

[9] Ibid., p. 99.

[10] Ibid., pp. 102-3.

[11] Ibid., p. 103.

[12] Ibid.

[13] Ibid., p. 158.

[14] Ibid., pp. 142-3.

[15] Ibid., p. 160.

[16] Ibid.

[17] Ibid., p. 188.

[18] Ibid., p. 190.

[19] Ibid., p. 197.

[20] Ibid., p. 199.

[21] Ibid.

[22] Ibid., pp. 201-2.

[23] William Perkins, Christian Oeconomie (London: Printed for Leonard Greene and Felix Kingstone, 1618), p. 669.

[24] Ibid., p. 671.

[25] Ibid.

[26] Ibid., p. 687.

[27] Ibid., p. 688.

[28] Cf. Henre Smith, p. 61 above.

[29] William Gouge, Of Domesticall Duties (London: Printed by John Haviland, 1622), p. 215.

[30] Ibid., p. 225.

[31] Ibid., pp. 238-9.

[32] Ibid., p. 240.

[33] Ibid., p. 243.

[34] Daniel Rogers, *Matrimoniall Honor: or The Mutuall Crowne and Comfort of Godly, Loyall, and Chaste Marriage* (London: Printed by Th:Harper, MDCXLII), p. 71.

[35] Ibid., p. 128.

[36] Ibid., p. 129

[37] Ibid.

[38] Ibid., p. 130

[39] Ibid., p. 131.

[40] John Milton, "Tetrachordon" in *Complete Prose Works of John Milton*, II, ed. Ernest Sirluck (New Haven: Yale University Press, 1959), 598. Hereafter cited as *Tetra*.

[41] John Milton, "The Doctrine and Discipline of Divorce," in *Complete Prose Works of John Milton*, II, ed. Ernest Sirluck (New Haven: Yale University Press, 1959), 249. Hereafter cited as *DDD*.

[42] *DDD*, p. 340.

[43] *DDD*, pp. 235-6.

[44] *DDD*, p. 260.

[45] See "Translator's Introduction" in D. W. Robertson's translation of St. Augustine's *De Doctrina Christiana* (New York: The Bobbs-Merrill Company, Inc., 1958), xi.

[46] *DDD*, p. 242.

[47] DDD, p. 329.

[48] William R. Parker, Milton: A Biography (Oxford: At the Clarendon Press, 1968), p. 243.

[49] Ibid.

[50] Ibid.

[51] DDD, p. 244.

[52] DDD, cf. Etiènne Gilson's comments quoted in Chapter II above, n. 33, p. 33.

[53] DDD, p. 245.

[54] DDD, p. 246.

[55] DDD, p. 248.

[56] DDD, p. 249.

[57] DDD, p. 252. cf. Plato's comments quoted above from The Symposium, n. 19, p. 26 (Chapter II).

[58] See Chapter II above, n. 20, p. 27.

[59] DDD, p. 259.

[60] DDD, p. 276.

[61] DDD, p. 277.

[62] DDD, p. 303.

[63] DDD, pp. 330-31.

[64] DDD, p. 309.

[65] DDD, p. 320.

[66] DDD, p. 331.

[67] DDD, p. 333.

[68] DDD, p. 339.

[69] DDD, p. 339.

[70] DDD, p. 343.

[71] DDD, p. 356.

[72] Parker, op. cit., p. 244.

[73] Arnold Williams, "Preface and Notes to Tetrachordon," Complete Prose Works of John Milton, II, ed. Ernest Sirluck (New Haven: Yale University Press, 1959), 571.

[74] Parker, op. cit., p. 281.

[75] Tetra., pp. 587-88.

[76] Tetra., p. 591.

[77] Tetra., cf. Milton's sixth reason for the law of divorce, p. 626. There might be some contradiction. However, in this passage, Milton still thinks that a woman may divorce an unfit husband, but it must be understood that the first permission of divorce was not given for the sake of woman--she is just being mercifully included.

[78] Tetra., p. 595.

[79] Tetra., p. 598.

[80] Tetra., p. 599.

[81] The irrationality of coupling two ill-natured persons is a theme that Milton stresses. In fact, this theme is one of his main lines of defense, along with the "rule of charity."

[82] Tetra., p. 604.

[83] *Tetra.*, p. 614.

[84] *Tetra.*, pp. 621-31.

[85] *Tetra.*, p. 623.

[86] *Tetra.*, p. 624.

[87] *Tetra.*, p. 625.

[88] *Tetra.*, pp. 630, 631.

[89] *Tetra.*, p. 637.

[90] *Tetra.*, p. 639.

[91] *Tetra.*, p. 646.

[92] *Tetra.*, p. 649.

[93] *Tetra.*, p. 650.

[94] *Tetra.*, p. 663.

[95] *Tetra.*, p. 665.

[96] *Tetra.*, p. 678.

[97] *Tetra.*, p. 681.

[98] *Tetra.*, p. 682.

[99] *Tetra.*, p. 683.

[100] *Tetra.*, p. 686.

[101] *Tetra.*, p. 686.

[102] *Tetra.*, p. 687.

[103] John Milton, *De Doctrina Christiana* in *The Works of John Milton*, XVI, gen. ed. Frank Allen Patterson (New York: Columbia

University Press, 1934), 142-45. Hereafter cited as DDC.

[104] DDC, p. 120.

[105] DDC, pp. 596, 597.

[106] DDC, p. 155.

[107] DDC, p. 176.

Chapter IV

[1] All quotations from Paradise Lost are taken from Merritt Y. Hughes' edition of John Milton: Complete Poems and Major Prose (New York: The Odyssey Press, 1957), pp. 207-469. Hereafter cited as CP.

[2] See Chap. II, n. 3.

[3] DDD, Book I, Chapter XIII, p. 275.

[4] See Chap. III, n. 43.

[5] Ibid., n. 44.

[6] Ibid.

[7] DDD, Book I, Chapter VI, p. 256.

[8] See Chap. II, n. 5.

[9] Mary Ann Radzinowicz, "'Man as a Probationer of Immortality': Paradise Lost XI-XII," in Approaches to Paradise Lost, ed. C. A. Patrides (London: Edward Arnold, Ltd., 1968), p. 36.

[10] The last two books of Paradise Lost are traditionally interpreted as a lesson to Adam on the meaning of death.

[11] Stella P. Revard, "Eve and the Doctrine of Responsibility in Paradise Lost," PMLA, Vol. 88, No. I (January, 1973), p. 76.

[12] George Williamson, "The Education of Adam" in *Milton and Others* (London: Faber and Faber, 1965), p. 47.

[13] C. S. Lewis, *Preface to Paradise Lost*, 7th ed. (London, New York, Toronto: Oxford University Press, 1952), p. 123.

[14] There are two ways of interpreting the term "native home," as it relates to usage in the works of St. Augustine and of Milton. St. Augustine, in *De Doctrina Christiana*, refers to man's "native country" as Heaven. Milton, in the above reference to man's "native home," is thinking in terms of man's creation from the dust of the earth, but he also insinuates Heaven, as is implied in Book VII, 154-61. For an understanding of Milton's concepts of mortalism, see his *De Doctrina Christiana*, Book I, Chapter XIII. For some knowledge of the possible controversy that can develop around this concept, see "Milton's Mortalism: Treatise vs. Poetry" in *Seventeenth Century News*, Vol. 26, No. 3, Item 4 (Autumn, 1968), pp. 51-52.

[15] Radzinowicz, *op. cit.*, p. 39.

[16] *Ibid.*, p. 37.

Chapter V

[1] See Chap. III, nn. 74 and 75.

[2] All quotations from *Samson Agonistes* are taken from Merritt Y. Hughes' edition of *John Milton: Complete Poems and Major Prose* (New York: The Odyssey Press, 1957), pp. 549-93. Hereafter cited as CP.

[3] Michael Krouse, *Milton's Samson and the Christian Tradition* (Princeton: Princeton University Press, 1949), p. 31.

[4] *Ibid.*, pp. 35-6.

⁵Ibid., p. 36.

⁶Ibid.

⁷Ibid., p. 34.

⁸Ibid., p. 36.

⁹Daton Haskin, S. J., "Divorce as a Path to Union with God in Samson Agonistes," ELH, Vol., 38, No. 3 (September, 1971), p. 367.

¹⁰See Chap. II, n. 5.

¹¹Ibid., n. 7.

¹²See Chap. III, n. 44.

¹³Ibid., n. 60.

¹⁴See Chap. II, n. 25.

¹⁵See CP, p. 564.

¹⁶Tetra., pp. 681-2.

¹⁷William R. Parker, Milton: A Biography (Oxford: At the Clarendon Press, 1968), p. 347. For sources suggesting that the Samson-Harapha confrontation is symbolic of the Milton-Salmasius philosophical battle, see Merritt Y. Hughes' introduction to Samson Agonistes in Complete Poems and Major Prose, p. 535, fn. 15.

¹⁸Haskin, op. cit., p. 358.

¹⁹Ibid., p. 359.

²⁰Ibid., p. 361.

Chapter VI

[1] H. Huftier, <u>La Charité Dans L'Enseignement De Saint Augustin</u>, V (Tournai, Paris, Rome, New York: Desclée, 1959), 5.

[2] <u>Ibid</u>.

[3] Henri Marrou, <u>Saint Augustine</u>, trans. Patrick Hepbourne-Scott (London: Longmans, 1957), p. 197.

[4] <u>DDD</u>, Book II, Chap. XII.

Bibliography

Augustini, Sancti Aurelii. De Doctrina Christiana in Opera Omnia. Vol. 4. Parisiis: Apud Gaume Fratres, Bibliopolas, M DCCC XXXVI.

Augustini, Sancti Aurelii. Enchiridion De Fide, Spe et Charitate in Opera Omnia. Vol. 3, Pt. I. Parisiis: Apud Gaume Fratres, Bibliopolas, M DCCC XXXVII.

Augustini, Sancti Aurelii. In Joannis Evangelium in Opera Omnia. Vol. 3, Pt. 2. Parisiis: Apud Gaume Fratres, Bibliopolas, M DCCC XXXVII.

Barker, Arthur. "Christian Liberty in Milton's Divorce Pamphlets," MLR, XXXV (April, 1940), pp. 153-61.

Barker, Arthur. Milton and the Puritan Dilemma: 1641-1660. Canada: The University of Toronto Press, 1942.

Burnaby, John. Amor Dei: A Study of the Religion of St. Augustine. London: Hudder and Stoughton, 1938.

Cleaver, Robert. A Godlie Forme of Householde Government: for the Ordering of Private Families According to the Direction of Gods Word. London: Printed by Felix Kingston, 1598.

Daiches, David. Milton. London: Hutchinson University Library, 1957.

Diekhoff, John S. Milton on Himself. New York: Oxford University Press, 1939.

Dodge, R. E. Neil, ed. The Complete Poetical Works of Spenser. Massachusetts: The Riverside Press, 1936.

Gilson, Etiènne. Introduction à L'Etude De Saint Augustin. Paris: Librairie Philosophique, J. Vrin, 1929.

Gouge, William. Of Domesticall Duties. London: Printed by John Haviland, 1622.

Halkett, George. Milton and the Idea of Matrimony. New Haven: Yale University Press, 1970.

Haller, William. "Hail Wedded Love," ELH, XIII (June, 1946), 27-97.

Haller, William. Liberty and Reformation in the Puritan Revolution. New York: The Columbia University Press, 1955.

Hanford, James Holly. "The Chronology of Milton's Private Studies," PMLA, XXXVI (March, 1921), 251-314.

Haskin, S. J., Daton. "Divorce as a Path to Union with God in Samson Agonistes," ELH, XXXVIII (September, 1971), 358-76.

Huftier, M. La Charité Dans L'Enseignement De Saint Augustin. Vol. 5. Tournai, Paris, Rome, New York: Desclée, 1959.

Huguelet, Theodore L. Milton's Hermeneutics: A Study of Scriptural Interpretation in the Divorce Tracts and in De Doctrina Christiana. Diss. University of North Carolina, 1959.

Knight, W. S. M. The Life and Works of Hugo Grotius. London: Sweet & Maxwell, limited, 1925.

Krouse, Michael. Milton's Samson and the Christian Tradition. Princeton: Princeton University Press, 1949.

Larson, Martin A. The Modernity of Milton. Chicago, Illinois: The University of Chicago Press, 1927.

Lewis, C. S. Preface to Paradise Lost. 7th ed. London, New York, Toronto: Oxford University Press, 1952.

Masson, David. The Life of John Milton. Vol. 3. New York: Peter Smith, 1946.

Milton, John. "An Apology for Smectymnuus" in John Milton: Complete Poems and Major Prose. Ed. Merritt Y. Hughes. New York: The Odyssey Press, 1957.

Milton, John. De Doctrina Christiana in The Works of John Milton. Vol. 16. Gen. ed. Frank Allen Patterson. New York: Columbia University Press, 1934.

Milton, John. The Doctrine and Discipline of Divorce in Complete Prose Works of John Milton. Vol. 2. Ed. Ernest Sirluck. New Haven: Yale University Press, 1959.

Milton, John. Paradise Lost in John Milton: Complete Poems and Major Prose. Ed. Merritt Y. Hughes. New York: The Odyssey Press, 1957.

Milton, John. Samson Agonistes in John Milton: Complete Poems and Major Prose. Ed. Merritt Y. Hughes. New York: The Odyssey Press, 1957.

Milton, John. Tetrachordon in Complete Prose Works of John Milton. Vol. 2. Ed. Ernest Sirluck. New Haven: Yale University Press, 1959.

Oates, Whitney J., ed. Basic Writings of Saint Augustine. Vol. 1. New York: Random House Publishers, 1948.

Parker, William R. Milton: A Biography. Vol. 1. Oxford: Clarendon Press, 1968.

Patrides, C. A. Milton and the Christian Tradition. Oxford: Clarendon Press, 1966.

Perkins, William. Christian Oeconomie. London: Printed for Leonard Greene and Felix Kingston, 1618.

Plato. "Symposium," Great Books of the Western World. Vol. 7. Chicago: William Benton, 1952.

Potts, James Basil. Milton's Deviations from Standard Biblical Interpretation in the Discussion of Divorce. Diss. University of Mississippi, 1968.

Powell, Chilton L. "The Date and Occasion of Milton's First Divorce Tract," English Domestic Relations: 1482-1653. New York: The Columbia University Press, 1917.

Radzinowicz, Mary Ann. "'Man as a Probationer of Immortality': Paradise Lost XI-XII," in Approaches to Paradise Lost. Ed. C. A. Patrides. London: Edward Arnold, Ltd., 1968.

Revard, Stella P. "Eve and the Doctrine of Responsibility in *Paradise Lost*." *PMLA*, LXXXVIII (January, 1973), 69-78.

Robertson, D. W., Jr., trans. *On Christian Doctrine* by St. Augustine. New York: The Bobbs-Merrill Company, Inc., 1958.

Rogers, Daniel. *Matrimoniall Honor: or the Mutuall Crowne and Comfort of Godly, Loyall, and Chaste Marriage*. London: Printed by Th:Harper, M DC XLII.

Samuel, Irene. *Plato and Milton*. New York: The Odyssey Press, 1947.

Saurat, Denis. *Milton, Man, and Thinker*. London: J. M. Dent and Sons Ltd., 1946.

Schaff, Philip, ed. *Homilies on the Gospel of St. John. Homilies on the First Epistle of John. Soliloquies* by St. Augustine. New York: The Christian Literature Company, 1888.

Sidney, Sir Philip. *Defense of Poesy*. Ed. Dorothy M. Marcardle. London: Macmillan & Co., Ltd; New York: St. Martin's Press, 1963.

Smith, Henre. "Preparative to Marriage," *The Sermons of Maister Henre Smith*. London: Printed by Felix Kingston, 1597.

Tillyard, E. M. W. *Milton*. London: Chatto and Winders, 1956.

University of Chicago. *Encyclopedia Britannica*. Vol. 2. Chicago, Illinois: William Benton, 1972.

Williamson, George. "The Education of Adam" in *Milton and Others*. London: Faber and Faber, 1965.